LEICESTER

Past and Present

LEICESTER

Past and Present

JACK SIMMONS

VOLUME TWO

Modern City

1860–1974

EYRE METHUEN
London

FIRST PUBLISHED 1974
© 1974 JACK SIMMONS
PRINTED IN GREAT BRITAIN FOR
EYRE METHUEN LTD
11 NEW FETTER LANE, LONDON EC4P 4EE
BY COX AND WYMAN LTD
FAKENHAM AND READING
ISBN 0 413 30890 1

Contents

Illustrations

MAPS

Acknowledgements and thanks for permission to reproduce photographs are due to the City of Leicester Publicity Department for plates 1, 2a, 11b and 16b; to the City of Leicester Museums for plates 5b, 8a, 9a, 9b, 10a and 14b; to the University of Leicester for plates 12, 17a and 22a; to the City Architect's Department for plate 19a; to *The Leicester Mercury* for plates 4 and 18b; to Leicester City Libraries for plates 8b and 13; to the National Monuments Record (Crown Copyright) for plates 3, 14a, 15, 21a, 21b and 23a; to the National Westminster Bank for plate 7b; to Thomas Cook & Son Ltd for plate 10a; to the Midland Camera Co. for plate 7b; to Zarb Photographers for plate 19b; to the British Museum for plate 23b; to Aerofilms Ltd for plates 17b and 20; to Frank Joseph for plate 24a; to W. J. Toomey for plate 24b; to the Air Ministry for plate 18a. Plates 5a and 22b are from photographs by the author.

The same acknowledgements are due to Routledge & Kegan Paul in respect of maps 3 and 4; to the Victoria History of the Counties of England for map 5; to Adam & Charles Black for map 1 (from Black's *Guide to Leicestershire*, 1885). Maps 2, 6 and 7 were drawn by Neil Hyslop, from originals by the author.

Abbreviations

Billson	C. J. Billson, *Medieval Leicester* (1920)
BM	British Museum
Ellis	Isabel C. Ellis, *Records of Nineteenth Century Leicester* (1935)
LM	*Leicester Mercury*
LPA	Local and Personal Acts
LRL	Leicester City Reference Library
LRLP	Leicester City Reference Library: Collection of Local Pamphlets
Mayors	Henry Hartopp, *Roll of the Mayors and Lord Mayors of Leicester* (1932)
PP	*Parliamentary Papers* (the pagination given is that of the set in BM)
RBL	*Records of the Borough of Leicester*, ed. Mary Bateson, Helen Stocks, and G. A. Chinnery (7 vols, 1899–1974)
RLDM	*Reports of the Leicester Domestic Mission* (in LRL)
RMOH	*Reports of the Medical Officer of Health* (in LRL)
Read	Robert Read, *Modern Leicester* (1881)
Region	*Leicester and its Region*, ed. N. Pye (1972)
Storey	John Storey, *Historical Sketch of some of the Principal Works and Undertakings of the Council of the Borough of Leicester* (1895)
TLAS	*Transactions of the Leicestershire Archaeological Society*
VCH	*Victoria History of the Counties of England*
VCHL	*Victoria History of the County of Leicester* (5 vols published, 1907–64)

Preface

This volume concludes my study of Leicester, taking the story from about 1860, when a major economic change became apparent in the town, to 1 April 1974, when the County Borough ceased to exist as such and Leicester became a District within the new County Council. The general purpose of the book is indicated in my earlier Preface, and I have also recorded there my chief obligations for assistance of various sorts kindly rendered to me in the preparation of both volumes.

I have used one term quite often here, which perhaps needs to be explained: 'the Old Town'. By that I mean the town within the line of its medieval walls, the near-rectangle (indicated in the map on page 20 of the first volume) bounded by Sanvey Gate, Churchgate, Gallowtree Gate, Horsefair Street, the Newarke, and the river.

Cross-references to the first volume appear throughout in the abbreviated form: 'i.140'.

The University   J. S.
Leicester
16 May 1974

LEICESTER

Past and Present

I
Prosperity

The Leicester of 1860 was still a small town in its scale. At the census of 1861, 68,000 people lived within the limits of the borough boundaries, and that gave it the twentieth place among the towns of the English provinces. Though it was now very much a centre of industry, it had not grown with the same speed as the Lancashire cotton towns: it was still at this time smaller than Bolton, Oldham, and Preston. Nottingham stood ahead of it, and so did Norwich.[1]

The ancient walls had gone, and the gates had been pulled down in 1774 (i.117–18), but they still exercised an unseen power: for the majority of those 68,000 people lived within their limits or immediately beyond them, huddled tightly together in the old lath-and-plaster houses or in close streets of new red brick. It was a town with a long past, adapting itself to a bewildering present and a highly uncertain future.

The 1850s, though they had had their ups and downs (i.166), had on the whole been a more cheerful time than the preceding decades. But there could be no confidence in a higher level of continuous employment, and therefore of general prosperity, unless the town's economic structure could be broadened. It was enslaved to the hosiery trade. Until other industries were established, it was tied to one that, in a contemporary epigram, 'barely subsists the operative, and does not enrich the merchant';[2] an industry whose prosperity varied most dangerously from one year to another, for reasons beyond its own control. Thoughtful people had long understood that the economy of the town could not become stable, still less prosperous, until other industries had established themselves by its side.[3] That is what began to happen about 1860.

[1] For a comparison with other towns in 1801 see i.140–1.
[2] Sir Richard Phillips, *Personal Tour through the United Kingdom* [1828], 76.
[3] Cf. 7 RLDM 6.

I

We cannot say precisely when or how the mechanised manufacture of boots and shoes came to be introduced into Leicester. Its development did more than anything else to cure the central weakness in the town's economy. The importance of the change was obvious, and recognised at once. Yet the emergence of the new manufacture is a tangled and obscure story,[1] and one element of myth enters into it at the outset, imported by that august and matter-of-fact body the Census Commissioners.

There had long been a large number of shoemakers in the town – perhaps more than were needed to satisfy purely local demands. Two wholesale shoemakers are recorded in 1835, and one of these, Thomas Crick, is a figure of outstanding note, for he adopted machine-riveting and by about 1855 was using steam power. The number of men and women employed in the making of boots and shoes grew fast. In 1841 it was 764. Twenty years later it was 3,206; in 1871, 5,003.

Commenting on the size of this last figure, the Superintendent Registrar of the Census attributed it to a strike at Northampton that 'about the year 1861 ... caused the removal of a large portion of its shoe trade to Leicester',[2] and that story has often been repeated since. A grain of truth is to be found in the tale, but mixed with such a quantity of chaff that we must call it, as a whole, a legend. There was indeed much unrest in the older centres of the shoemaking industry, Northampton and Stafford, in the 1850s, and a serious strike at Northampton in 1859. But the chief cause of all this trouble was the introduction of machinery into the manufacture. The last place to which these strikers would wish to move would surely be one that was distinguishing itself by the adoption of the very methods they were opposing. The industry was already established in Leicester, and on the new basis, in the 'fifties. Consider the history of Stead & Simpson's, who became one of the leading firms in the whole business. They began in the currying and leather trades at Leeds in 1834 and then went on to make shoes as a sideline. Ten years later they extended their interest into the Midlands, opening a branch at Daventry. They arrived in Leicester in 1853, still as curriers; but five years later they were sufficiently committed to shoemaking – and sufficiently enterprising – to adopt the Blake sole-sewing machine, a new American invention, and to pioneer the use of it in this country.

[1] It would repay a more exhaustive investigation than it has yet received. Meanwhile, there is a useful summary of what is at present known in VCHL iv.314–9. See also A. Granger, *History of the Boot and Shoe Industry in Leicester* (1965).
[2] PP. 1872 lxvi, pt ii, 344.

The disturbances in the industry at Northampton and Stafford did unquestionably benefit Leicester, as well as Kendal, which became a shoemaking town at the same time. Soon – what an irony! – the employers in Northampton were sending their men to Leicester to learn the new methods at Crick's.[1] The census figures give us a clear hint of what happened. The number of people born in Northamptonshire and living in Leicester showed an insignificant increase in the 'fifties. In 1861–71 it rose from 1,926 to 3,077; in the next ten years to 4,605.

But no Northampton strike established the manufacture of footwear in Leicester. It was established, and made its first growth, independently.

In the 'sixties the industry continued to grow, and fast. By 1861 there were twenty-three wholesale manufacturers of boots and shoes in Leicester, most of them we can be sure small men. Their number had increased to 117 by 1870. In 1881 Leicester was employing 25 per cent more people in the industry than Northampton, its original metropolis; and it remained ahead for the next fifty years. Thomas Crick continued for a time to be the biggest man in the trade; his works in Southgate Street were extended in 1862.[2] But other names, better known today, now came to stand side by side with his. George Oliver's, for example. He was a Leicestershire man, apprenticed first to a shoemaker at Barrow-on-Soar and then, in the 1860s, opening shops for the sale of shoes in Staffordshire. For a short time he manufactured at Wolverhampton. In 1875 he made up his mind to concentrate entirely on distribution, closed his factory and opened a large warehouse in Leicester, whence he served thirty branches. By 1889 those thirty had become 100, and he claimed to be the largest retailer of boots and shoes anywhere in the world.

Oliver's business grew on a pattern that came to be typical of Leicester, with a strong emphasis on distribution as well as, or in place of, manufacture. There was nothing accidental in that. As a distributive centre, Leicester was excellently placed, at the heart of a good railway system, which became rapidly better in these years (see Map 6). By contrast Northampton stood forlornly on branch lines until 1882, and even then, when it had been placed on a secondary main line, its communication with the North-East and with Wales and the West remained much inferior to Leicester's.

The new industry was in some respects remarkably like its partner the hosiery business. Though eventually it threw up a few firms that became nationally known, like the two that have been mentioned and Freeman Hardy & Willis, these were never characteristic. It was the small firm that, here again, predominated. Only a little capital was needed to set up in business, since nearly all the machinery could be hired. Again, here is a close similarity to the hosiery trade. The normal firm

[1] VCH Northants., ii. 327–8.
[2] 2 TLAS (1870) 175.

3

was a small unit, the proprietor managing it with other members of his family. If he was successful, he became comfortable enough; but he was still in no large way of business. One practice in the shoe manufacture derived directly from the hosiery trade: letting out machines to domestic workers in the surrounding villages. Many of them were women, who preferred to work in their own homes rather than in the confined and often unpleasant conditions of a factory.

All the same, the parallel between the two trades was not exact, and in one respect they became diametrical opposites. The hosiery industry had always employed a large number of women. That had had certain social advantages. But, on balance, it had been a weakness, one of the forces that had kept wages low and depressed the spirit of the men, the heads of families. Although there was much work for women in the manufacture of footwear, it was predominantly a man's trade. As time went on and the two industries settled down together, they came to complement each other most happily: so that in 1881 we find women preponderating over men in hosiery in the ratio of 5:3 and men preponderating over women in footwear by 9:4.

Both industries became, though at no rapid pace, more elaborately mechanised; and their demands played some part in bringing about another great economic development – the growth of an engineering industry in Leicester.[1] We have noted (i.132) that there were ironfounders in the town from the late eighteenth century onwards. Among them Corts' remained pre-eminent, not only in the business they transacted but, perhaps even more, for the young men they trained as apprentices. A number of these established small businesses of their own in the 1840s, which we can call engineering works. They tended at first to be closely linked to the local industries. Samuel and William Pegg, for example, began by supplying equipment to dyeworks in Leicester and to granite quarries in the county. In the second of these ventures they blazed a trail, followed by their rivals Goodwin Barsby and Parker. At the same time William Richards established his Phoenix Foundry, at first on the canal wharf and subsequently beside the Midland Railway. His business grew, later in the century, to specialise in heavy iron castings and steel work. He supplied, for example, the South Eastern Railway, and the inscription 'W. Richards & Son, makers, Leicester' is still to be seen on the piers supporting the platform roofs of that company's stations at London Bridge and Waterloo, and again conspicuously on a bridge over Belvedere Road, close to the Royal Festival Hall.

Among Corts' other apprentices were Benjamin and Josiah Gimson, members of a family very long established in Leicestershire. They come up as 'millwrights' in premises on the Welford Road in the early 1840s. Having passed through grave financial adversity, Josiah – a remarkable man, to be encountered again in another

[1] Cf. VCHL iii. 26–7.

connection – built the impressive Vulcan Works, adjoining the Midland Railway on its eastern side, in 1878.[1] Their establishment may be taken to mark the emergence of Leicester as an engineering town.

But it was engineering with a difference: for it always remained predominantly light engineering. One branch of the industry specialised in precision work, associated for example with T. J. Gent, who made telegraph instruments and electrical equipment of many kinds, above all clocks. Taylor Taylor & Hobson, a firm that attained international fame in the manufacture of lenses and optical goods, originated in a partnership of T. S. and William Taylor, brothers aged twenty-two and twenty-one, founded on a capital of £300 in 1886. Two years later they were joined by W. S. Hobson, and they achieved their first breakthrough when they began to make the Cooke photographic lens in 1893. In the First World War their lenses used in aerial reconnaissance work proved superior to the Germans'. Their reputation was made, and kept at all times, by the high quality of everything they produced.[2]

Another development of these years arose directly out of the industrial demands of Leicester. In the last quarter of the century it became the chief centre of production of the machinery required in the boot and shoe manufacture. The firm of Pearson & Bennion devoted itself to this work and achieved a pre-eminence in it. Then in 1899 it was swept up, together with other firms doing the same business in Britain, by the United Shoe Machinery Company of America. The new amalgamation became the British United Shoe Machinery Company, and its headquarters were established in Pearson & Bennion's Union Works in Belgrave Road. Though the original firm was an important concern, it was not yet a big one. It employed only 200 men and women at the time the Americans acquired it. In the twentieth century the new company grew to become one of the largest units of employment in the town.

The growth of the engineering industry has been, in the long run, as important for Leicester as that of the manufacture of boots and shoes. Immediately, it contributed much to the older-established industries, even though it may at times have irked them by competing for their labour. But in quantitative terms of employment its growth was much slower. The numbers engaged in the engineering and allied industries were less than 2,000 in 1891, less than 3,000 ten years later.

[1] For these works see 36 *Builder* (1878) 749 and Plate 6b.
[2] *Tally Ho – in Pursuit of Precision. The Taylor Taylor & Hobson Story, 1886–1956* [1956], 25–6.

2

Stimulated by these economic changes and becoming, with every year that passed, a more hopeful place to live in, Leicester grew in the 1860s faster than at any time before or since. In the 'fifties, when the improvement was in prospect rather than achieved, the increase of population had been 12·3 per cent, the lowest of any decade in the century. The growth in the 'sixties, by contrast, was staggering: by almost 40 per cent, from 68,000 to 95,000. In 1871 – for the first and only time in the history of the census – Leicester was bigger than Nottingham.

This increase was caused in large measure by immigration. The special case of the shoe trade has been discussed, but it did not stand alone. The deep depression that hit the Coventry ribbon trade about 1860 caused people there to look elsewhere for work. They are said to have found it in part in the elastic web manufacture of Leicester.[1] Certainly the number of Warwickshire-born people in the town increased more than $2\frac{1}{2}$ times over in that decade. We can get an idea of the scale of immigration from the fall in the number of those born in Leicestershire. In the 'sixties this showed a decrease from 80·5 per cent of the town's population to 76·6 – the largest change in any decennial period for which information is available. Looking ahead, it is worth noting that that percentage continued to decline until the end of the century, when it began to rise again a little. It is impossible to say what happened after 1911, for at that point the useful information ceases. At no time during the years 1841–1911 was the proportion of Leicestershire-born people in the town as low as 70 per cent.

Here, then, in two successive decades the town grows at the slowest rate in the century and at the fastest. No simple cause, such as a change of boundaries, will account for that violent contrast. It can be explained in only one way: in terms of the changing opportunities of employment that Leicester could offer.

The first question we are likely to ask about this expansion is: where did all these people go to live? There had been 4·7 people to a house in 1861. Whatever must have been the number in 1871? The answer is that it was virtually the same – it had increased by 0·1 per cent. In other words, the 5,000 houses erected in Leicester within that decade kept pace with the demand. The density of occupation was, by our standards, far too high. It grew higher, and did not fall even a little until the first decade of the new century (perhaps then in part as a consequence of a boundary extension in 1892). That it grew no higher than it did is a tribute to the energy with which Mid-Victorian private enterprise threw itself into the task of building the streets and houses that were needed. Leicester certainly was a boom town for the builder and the tradesmen he employed. In 1865

[1] PP 1872 lxvi pt. ii, 344.

there were four times as many stonemasons in the town as there had been in the 1820s, and their wages were twice as high.[1] The number of men employed in the building trades more than doubled in 1861–81. The erection of all these houses was the work of private enterprise only. The Council did not concern itself in the business until after the First World War.

Let us look at this process in a little detail. We can trace – not only from documents, but also from maps, from the dates that very often the houses themselves carry still – the outward thrusts that the builders made, in seeking to satisfy the relentless demand they faced. Sometimes a whole new quarter was developed as a consequence of the sale of one or two large properties. In former days, for instance, there had never been any considerable suburb west of the river. Some industrial building appeared there – the Bow Bridge Mills in the 1820s, West Bridge Mills about 1848; and in the 'fifties a few houses followed along the Hinckley Road and Watts's Causeway, renamed King Richard's Road. But the total area built up was small. The desirable expansion lay up the slopes to the west, above the miasma and flooding of the river, and that could not come as long as the two old estates of Danet's Hall and Westcotes remained in private occupation. Danet's Hall, once lived in by the Watts family, had come into the hands of a well-known physician, Dr Noble. But he died suddenly, of cholera in Spain, in 1861. His estate was put up for sale, and bought by the Leicester Freehold Land Society. Building followed fast in what was grandly called the West End:[2] new streets, new houses, a striking new church (Ordish's St Paul's, brought into use in 1871), the new Wyggeston's Hospital, transferred to the Fosse Road from its original site in 1868. 'Noble Street' and 'Dannett Street' were all that were left as a reminder of the past. At the same time the Westcotes estate was being whittled away. 'Extremely chaste and beautiful Gothic schools'[3] were built on part of it in 1863. The manor house was sold in 1886. Westcotes Drive was cut through the estate, and all the higher ground above the Narborough Road was then available for building. The Narborough Road itself was developed, with a good many tall middle-class houses, as far as the railway bridge (Plate 9b). Beyond that lay the open country, little disturbed until after the First World War.

Or again, consider the Highfields. Although there were a number of ample houses on the London Road, as it rose up from Granby Street, the country lay open behind them to the east, apart from the Collegiate School of 1836 and the Union Workhouse (now Hillcrest), built two years later. But the school encouraged a little development, and the railway, when it was opened in 1840, a

---

[1] 23 *Builder* (1865) 838.
[2] 'West End Terrace 1864' is still to be seen on a large iron plate attached to a wall in the Hinckley Road.
[3] 2 TLAS (1870) 288.

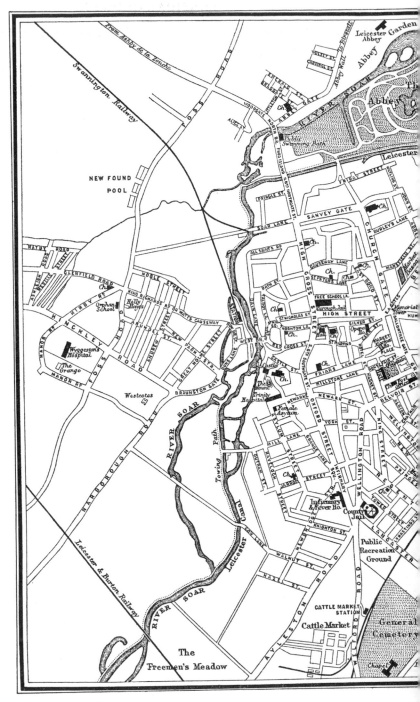

Leicester *c.* 1885

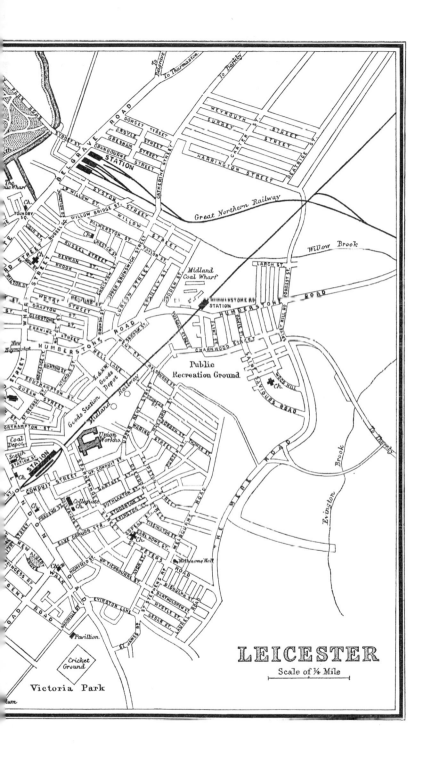

LEICESTER

Scale of ¼ Mile

good deal more. By 1857 Sparkenhoe Street was well built up; and, leading out of the London Road, Highfield Street and Mill Hill Lane.[1] In the 'sixties and 'seventies this gradually burgeoned into an airy, well-to-do suburb of tall houses, though the development did not get fully under way until Sparkenhoe Street and the London Road were linked. One sign of the district's prosperity was St Peter's church (cf. p. 46 and Plate 3), completed in 1879 and eschewing brick in favour of stone throughout; another was the opulent Melbourne Hall, built for the Rev. F. B. Meyer by his congregation in 1891; a third the arrival of the Synagogue in Highfield Street in 1898, to meet the needs of a Jewish community that had been growing, under the leadership of men like Israel Hart, since the 1860s. By a process characteristic of our time, this comfortable Mid-Victorian district has become one of the chief centres of the immigrant communities from the West Indies, from Africa and Asia.

It was suburbs like these that drew the development of the town out of the low-lying river valley. Though they were founded by and for the middle classes, they made the way very quickly for a parallel growth of artisan housing, and the whole community benefited.

3

In terms of bare number, the demands for new houses in the 'sixties and 'seventies were met; but they were often met badly, even disgracefully. In the 'forties the town contained no back-to-back houses. Those now became numerous. There were said to be 1,500 of them in 1864; certainly as late as the 1930s 300 survived, to be demolished in the energetic slum clearance of those years.[2] The Estates Committee of the new Corporation encouraged the vendors to impose stringent conditions on the purchasers of land sold for building. When the Local Board of Health was set up, it insisted that the plans of every new domestic or industrial building should be submitted to it. The intentions were good. But it proved impossible to realise them in practice.

There were four fundamental reasons for the Council's shortcomings, and they lie at the bottom of most of its deficiencies throughout the rest of the century. First, it was timid, unwilling to use its full powers to stop objectionable practices. Joseph Dare repeatedly drew attention, for example, to the prevalence of houses in Leicester in which the windows on the upper floor were not made to open. In one of them, during the torrid summer of 1851, he found a poor old widow who 'seemed to be literally frying in her bed, which was reeking with her perspiration'.

[1] Spencer's map, 1857 (i. 180–1).
[2] VCHL iv. 269, 291.

In 1864 he pointed out that many new houses were still being built with this dis-graceful defect.[1] The second shortcoming arose from the first. New houses, of some kind, were desperately needed. There was not time to argue thoroughly with those who sought to put them up. Nor was it only a matter of time. The third trouble was the inadequacy of the staff employed for the purpose. That could have been remedied if the Corporation had been willing to spend more freely; but – the story is an old one – it had much expensive work on hand, it feared the ratepayers' criticism, and it economised on staff. It appointed the first Borough Surveyor, to discharge these and a score of other duties, in 1849. At the same time it created the post of Officer of Health. (Leicester was the second town in the country to have such an officer, after Liverpool.) In John Moore, who served in that capacity from 1853 to 1867, it got a man recognised by competent observers to be 'zealous, able, and thoroughly efficient' and supported him well – whilst paying him a salary that the same observers condemned as 'miserably inadequate'.[2] How could such men, however devoted, watch all that they were supposed to oversee? The staff at their disposal was ludicrously small. No full-time Officer of Health was appointed until 1873; no Assistant until 1877.

And finally – perhaps most important of all – the Mid-Victorians were im-perfectly equipped, in many matters of knowledge and technique, to deal with the new problems that were confronting them with such formidable urgency. Those 27,000 people who were added to the population of Leicester in the 'sixties not only needed housing. They were obliged to share with the 68,000 who were already living in the town the main services, in so far as those were there at all. In particular, they had to have some supply of water, and they had to dispose of their sewage and refuse.

There was no piped water in the town until the 'fifties. All that was available was that provided by the Conduit, by the pumps set up in 1759 (i.122), by private wells, and by the river. The Conduit and the pumps, in a town of this size, were hardly more than quaint antiquities. The wells were often, for all sorts of reasons, polluted, and in the poorer quarters of the town each of them was shared between many users. The river was so filthy with household sewage and industrial effluent as to be for most purposes useless. There was no remedy except that of bringing in water from reservoirs outside. A private Waterworks Company was set up in 1846 to undertake the task, and in the following year it secured an Act authorising it to build a reservoir at Thornton, seven miles away to the north-west, and to pipe water thence into the town. But the capital proved impossible to raise until the Council, at the instigation of Joseph Whetstone, offered to go into partnership

[1] 7 RLDM 8; 19 RLDM 5.
[2] A. P. Stewart and E. Jenkins, *Medical and Legal Aspects of Sanitary Reform* (Victorian Library ed., 1971), 42.

with the Company, subscribing £17,000 of the £80,000 required and guarantee-ing a minimum dividend to the shareholders. The proposal evoked an outcry from some ratepayers, but an Act was obtained in 1851 to sanction it, and the work then went ahead. The first water from Thornton was brought into the town – appropriately, it was laid on to the Temperance Hall – on 21 December 1853.

It was a great step forward, but it soon proved inadequate to meet the demands of the growing population; and that was demonstrated by two dry summers in succession, in 1863 and 1864. A second reservoir was therefore constructed, under powers obtained in 1866, at Cropston. It was brought into use in 1870 and was designed to make the supply of water sufficient for a population of 160,000, even at a time of severe drought.[1] Again the Corporation contributed, by taking up part of the additional share capital; and in doing so it was making a profitable investment. By the 'seventies it began to consider exercising powers given to it under the original Acts to purchase the undertaking. In 1877 it took the plunge. It bought up the Leicester Gas Company; and later in the same year, after pro-tracted legal argument, the Water Company passed into its hands too.

Henceforward, the ratepayers were directly responsible for their water supply. It continued to be a good deal less than sufficient. A small 'service reservoir' was built at Oadby in 1885, to supply the fast-growing districts of Stoneygate and Clarendon Park, and the existing reservoirs were extended at the same time. Plans were laid for another at Swithland, but they were held up by long arguments, and the work was not begun until 1894. By that time another drought had caused serious trouble in the town, met in part by pumping water from Ellistown Colliery. The deficiencies of Leicester's water supply were now a matter of national notoriety. It was fortunate, said the *Builder* in a rude leading article, that the citizens were content, even in normal times, to consume so little: 'we shudder to think how much more sorely taxed the Corporation might have been were the first principles of hygiene occasionally resorted to by the bulk of the inhabitants'.[2]

The crisis was tided over. But even the Swithland reservoir was not enough, and the Corporation had to look further afield. It turned to the Derwent valley in Derbyshire, and in collaboration with Derby, Nottingham, and Sheffield con-structed a large reservoir there, which was completed in 1912. Then at last the supply was judged adequate, for a whole generation to come.

Only a minority of people in Leicester had baths in their houses. The Corpora-tion had for a long time helped to provide public baths. From 1849 onwards it subsidised two privately-owned establishments, on condition that they offered cheap bathing facilities. Then in 1879 it built its own baths, in Bath Lane, followed by a second set in Vestry Street twelve years later. It also provided

[1] 13 *Engineering* (1872) 431–2.
[2] 67 *Builder* (1894) 273.

bathing places on the river in 1867–8,[1] though in view of the appalling condition of the water we may doubt if they were, on balance, of much benefit. Still, they augmented amusement – very often, admittedly, at the expense of decency;[2] and that gain, imponderable as it was, ought not to be despised.

The river presented the Corporation with what was in many ways the most difficult challenge it now had to meet, and certainly in the end the most expensive. In the past it had been the town's greatest friend. Leicester owed its very origin to the Soar, as well as a handsome contribution to its economic growth. But the river had always been liable to serious flooding, which restricted the use of otherwise valuable building land on its banks. And by the middle of the nineteenth century it had come to be, from one cause and another, a fertile source of disease.

There was no sewerage system before 1850. Such sewers as there were had been constructed by the parish authorities, or by private developers laying out new streets, or sometimes by both in collaboration. They followed no general plan, and they were largely ineffective. For want of sufficient fall their contents tended simply to accumulate and become noisome at a point of blockage. In so far as they did discharge, it was invariably into the river.

The new Local Board of Health set itself at once to make the provision that was so urgently required. In 1849 it commissioned Thomas Wicksteed to report on the whole problem and two years later it adopted his proposals for establishing a system of sewers and for treating, by a patent process in which he was himself interested, the matter that passed through them. The work was put in hand and completed by 1855. Although it effected a considerable improvement, it was criticised by Edwin Chadwick with his habitual asperity, and the criticism was well founded. In the course of the 'sixties, as the system came to be more and more overloaded, its deficiencies grew horribly plain. During some of the hot summers of that decade, the stench arising from the Soar became unbearable, and the 'summer diarrhoea' that rendered the town notorious (in 1868 there were four times as many deaths from that malady in Leicester as in the whole of London)[3] was generally attributed to this cause. The Corporation had already spent £45,000 on Wicksteed's scheme and on necessary extensions to it.[4] Naturally it resisted the notion that a wholly new system would have to be substituted. It was caught in a cross-fire of experts, for sanitary engineering had by no means become an exact science. We must sympathise with it a little in its perplexities, though much more with the citizens who suffered the consequences of the engineers' imperfect knowledge and mistakes. For a moment, in 1871, Leicester had the highest

[1] 23 RLDM 4.
[2] 16 RLDM 16; 24 *ibid.* 10.
[3] 27 *Builder* (1869) 249.
[4] Storey, 13–14.

death-rate of any town in the country: 'a mortality from one disease alone higher than that of Bombay from every cause whatsoever!'[1]

The trouble did not arise only from the insufficiency of the sewers. It was due also to the limitations of the supply of water. The Water Company imposed its own restrictions. The use of water-closets was spreading steadily, but the Company refused to supply any house for that purpose alone.[2] This rule seriously restricted the general sanitary benefit the water-closet offered, helping to preserve in use cesspools and earth privies that would otherwise have been replaced. (All the same, the number of water-closets in Leicester was high, by comparison with other towns of the same sort.[3] In 1868 it had one to every twelve inhabitants, twice as many in proportion as Nottingham or Liverpool, six times as many as Leeds, thirteen times as many as Sheffield.) At this point the Local Board organised a 'pail-closet' system, on a model that had been found acceptable in Rochdale and elsewhere. Some 7,000 of these closets were eventually brought into use in the town, and they provided a welcome alleviation; but the removal of the contents of each through the streets on to railway wagons or barges on the river was a stinking and filthy incident of the night, and the practice was only too plainly a confession of defeat.

Meanwhile, the sewerage system remained unaltered. Plan and counter-plan were put forward; inquiries were held, and every proposal was turned to ridicule by its rivals. An irrigation scheme was now widely preferred to Wicksteed's unsuccessful system of turning the sewage into saleable manure, and by 1873 it was perceived that any effective solution to the problem must provide for three things in conjunction: for better sewers, for carrying away storm waters, and for greatly improving the river, so as to eliminate the flooding to which it was constantly subject. A series of minor improvements was effected in 1877, but still the main work was delayed – and, as usual, the longer it was delayed the higher the cost of it grew. It would be wrong to attribute the failure to act to the parsimony of the Corporation. At no point was a comprehensive plan agreed, and then rejected as too expensive. The Corporation's mental attitude in the matter was not one of mere conservatism or stupidity; its characteristic was bewilderment. It may perhaps be unjust to lay the chief blame on the Borough Surveyor, E. L. Stephens. But when placed on the defensive, his public apologies tended to seem weak,[4] and a marked change for the better appeared when, on his death in 1880, he was succeeded by Joseph Gordon.

Gordon was a man of unquestionable brilliance who might well have attained a

[1] 29 *Builder* (1871) 779.
[2] RMOH 1855, 10.
[3] RMOH 1868, 21–2.
[4] Cf., for example, 27 *Builder* (1869) 281; 29 *ibid.* (1871) 901.

reputation comparable with that of Thomas Hawksley, the great water engineer of Nottingham, or Sir Joseph Bazalgette, to whom London owes a debt that is beyond computation. He had had wide and various experience before he came to Leicester, first in England at Carlisle and then on the Continent, especially at Frankfurt. The Corporation of Leicester certainly went to the top when it chose him. He served it for nine years, and though he could not cut through the tangle of difficulties he confronted, a long-term solution to them was evolved, to plans prepared by him. The work of constructing a fresh system of main sewers was at last begun in 1886; an entirely new pumping station, with irrigation works, was brought into use at Beaumont Leys from 1890 onwards. The number of pail-closets began to diminish, and in 1895 the Corporation was able to ordain their complete discontinuance. By 1900 Leicester had not only a new sewerage system but one that was good enough to serve it without any major change for fifty years.

At the same time the improvement of the river had also been carried through to its end. It was first taken in hand with real energy in 1876, and completed in 1891. The 'Flood Prevention Scheme', as it was generally called, was on a bigger scale even than the sewerage system. It cost, all told, about £300,000 and involved the widening and deepening of the river, cutting new channels for it, rebuilding the West Bridge of 1841 with a larger span and providing three new bridges to the south. In the past nearly a fifth of the town's population had been subjected to flooding.[1] Now that curse was removed.

Taken together, the sewerage and river works represent Town Improvement in its most decisive and incontestable form. Although the sewers themselves remain buried (as they should), the whole achievement has two striking memorials that are visible above ground. One is the course of the main river to be seen today, an artificial cut stretching trimly southward from the West Bridge, for almost a mile dead straight. The other is the pumping station, now disused as such but happily handed over to form part of the city's new Museum of Technology. When one of its majestic beam engines, built by Gimson's, can be put back to work again, its tremendous pulsations will recall, as nothing else can, the engineers' triumph.

If the whole work took far too long, encountered many obstacles that should not have been placed in its way, and engendered much deplorable vituperation, it may yet be seen as a monument to the corporate pertinacity and patience of the Town Council and its committees. The central figure in it is Gordon. He left Leicester in 1889 for the post of Chief Engineer of the new London County Council – the highest appointment in the branch of the profession to which he belonged. Only two months later he died of heart failure, at the age of fifty-two.[2]

[1] Storey, 91.
[2] 57 *Builder* (1889) 353.

4

The shortcomings in the town's main services, and the remedies slowly worked out for them, closely reflect the changing condition of the people and their health. Here again the technology, in the treatment of disease, was very incompletely understood. It was almost as much a matter of experiment – experiment with the lives of human beings – as the evolution of a sound system of sewerage. Although the poor suffered most, they did not suffer alone. To take one example, a lady died in childbirth in one of the new houses up the hill to the west of the river in 1868, and it subsequently emerged that the drains in the house stopped in the garden, making no communication at all with the main sewer. The jerry-builder has been active at all times – though it was only in the Mid-Victorian age that a term came to be coined for him. In this instance he was a builder of good repute.[1]

When the close investigation of the health of British towns began, in the 1840s, Leicester's condition was deplorable. The death rate there in the years 1840–2 was 30:1000. For the country as a whole the average was 22:1000. The rate in Leicester was exceeded in Bristol, Liverpool, Manchester, and Hull alone. William Biggs's committee (i.170–1) attributed this severe mortality above all to the lack of a drainage system and to the foul state and flooding of the river; but it also drew attention to the poor physique of the people, who did not display 'the robust appearance visible even in the manufacturing districts of the North'. The mortality among infants was high: in 1841, 43·3 per cent of those who died in the town were children less than five years old.[2] These were indeed some of the worst years in the worst period of distress in Leicester's industrial history. The figures are a comment on them, and they give us a base-line to start from.

Three diseases came to stand out, at one time and another, as the principal killers in Leicester. First, typhus and typhoid fever, scourges of all the over-crowded and ill-built towns of the nineteenth century. A separate Fever House had been established at the Infirmary as early as 1820, accommodating about twenty-five patients. When there was a severe fever epidemic in the town in 1846 the Corporation besought the Infirmary to make additional provision to meet the emergency. The Infirmary felt obliged to refuse, suggesting instead that the parishes should set aside temporary fever houses themselves. The house surgeon died of it in 1848.[3] By that time, however, the virulence of the disease was les-

[1] Ellis, *Records*, 300.
[2] PP 1844 xvii. 506.
[3] Frizelle and Martin, *Leicester Royal Infirmary*, 100–2.

sening.[1] Fevers of all kinds were still dangerous; but they had come to be less prominent in people's minds than smallpox.

Though smallpox had long been a familiar enemy, its incidence now began to grow more alarming. After the town had been quite free of it for three or four years, it came back strongly in 1856. Next year, seventeen people died of it. Sixteen of those were unvaccinated,[2] and the immediate effect was to increase the demand for vaccination. The provision for nursing the disease was quite insufficient, since the Fever House declined to admit people suffering from it.[3] Dare gives us some terrible glimpses of its treatment in the homes he visited during the next epidemic, of 1863–4: of the dead body of the father of a family lying in the only bedroom of the house for three days before burial; of three children in bed together with the disease. One of those three died, having caught it from a child next door. Its mother had done nothing to stop them from meeting: 'I did not think it any use to keep my child away', she said, 'for God could find him out wherever he was, as well as He did the other'. No wonder Dare concluded that the worst failings of the poor were 'ignorance and filth and fatalism'.[4]

It was at this moment that the efficacy of vaccination began to be called into doubt. The practice grew in popularity in Leicester until 1864. In 1865 it suddenly slumped. True, the number of smallpox cases declined in that year; but the disease was still sufficiently prevalent to kill 120 people in the town in 1864–8. It was beginning to seem as if vaccination did not afford the security claimed for it. The vaccination of infants had been made obligatory by statute in 1853, but the law had not been strictly enforced. Now, in 1867, the earlier legislation was strengthened. An outcry arose, and nowhere was it heard louder than in Leicester, where it was efficiently organised by an Anti-Vaccination League, established in 1869.

The objectors' case rested on three arguments. First they contended that vaccination was ineffective. Second they believed, with some medical support, that it could cause diseases of the skin. And third they rejected, with all the force of the Nonconformist Liberalism that prevailed in their town, the principle of compulsion. It must have been a blow to them when Gladstone's strong Liberal administration passed another Act in 1871, reinforcing further the powers to require vaccination absolutely. In the epidemic that immediately followed, in 1871–2, the deaths in the town from smallpox rose to 314, the highest number ever recorded.

In 1869 the Board of Guardians, who were the responsible authority in the

[1] Cf. 16 RLDM 6.
[2] RMOH 1856, 6; 1857, 6–7.
[3] *Ibid.*, 1856, 7.
[4] 19 RLDM 14–16.

matter, began to prosecute parents who refused to have their children vaccinated. In the succeeding twenty years there were some 6,000 cases of the kind in Leicester, and sixty-four of the defendants went to prison rather than pay the fines that were imposed on them. This might appear to be nothing but an indefensible fuss, made by many of the parents on a quirk of principle, at the risk of their children's lives. But something more was involved. The objectors did not simply oppose vaccination. They offered an alternative treatment of the disease, by the strongest insistence on personal hygiene and by advocating immediate isolation not only of smallpox patients but also of those who had been in contact with them. They urged their arguments so strongly and coherently as to erect them into a system, which came to be known widely as 'the Leicester method'. It is this that gives the controversy its interest, even its importance: for in the end the Leicester objectors contributed something valuable to the practical treatment of the disease.

The first step in this direction had been taken by the Town Council. In 1869 it had begun to go into the business of providing hospitals of its own for specialised purposes, when it opened its lunatic asylum at Humberstone. Henceforth, patients from the borough were treated there, leaving the Leicestershire and Rutland Asylum (established south of the town in 1837) to serve the county. Two years later, in face of an epidemic of scarlet fever and fearing one of smallpox, it built an isolation hospital on Freak's Ground, immediately west of the river. Though this was something of a makeshift – the buildings were of corrugated iron – it continued in use until a permanent hospital was erected for the purpose in 1900, at Gilroes on the Groby Road.

When, therefore, the opponents of vaccination began to put forward their alternative methods of treating smallpox, the first and most necessary instrument for isolating patients was to hand. But they recognised that the acceptance of the principle of isolation was not enough: that it would have to be strictly enforced. This conclusion had already been reached and acted on elsewhere – for example at Huddersfield. At Leicester it was embodied in a private Act obtained by the Corporation in 1879,[1] requiring immediate notification of the disease, under penalty of a maximum fine of £10. It now became the regular practice, not only for the patient to be isolated but for all those who had been in close contact with him to be placed in quarantine; the disinfection of clothes, bedding, and rooms was also insisted on. The Guardians adopted this 'Leicester method' in place of enforcing vaccination. The town grew into a capital of the anti-vaccination cause. A great demonstration was held there in support of it in 1885, at which more than

[1] LPA 42 Vict. cap. 200, sect. 7. Huddersfield had gone further in 1876, making the removal of the patient to the fever hospital (when built) compulsory: LPA 39 Vict. cap. 100, sect. 65.

fifty towns were represented. One of the Members for the borough, P. A. Taylor, became its Parliamentary champion; and when he retired his successor J. A. Picton, lobbied relentlessly by the Leicester League, secured the appointment of a Royal Commission in 1889 to inquire into the working of the vaccination laws. Though the Commission's report did not go far enough to satisfy the opponents of vaccination, it led the Government to concede exemption from the practice, to be obtained by parents on grounds of conscience.

What happened in Leicester was indeed distinctive. In 1889 less than 4 per cent of the children born in the town were vaccinated; the law was a dead letter. Ten years later, when the post of vaccination officer fell vacant, the Guardians refused to fill it. They gave way only under the compulsion of a writ served on them at the instance of the central Government.

Meanwhile, what course had the disease taken in the town? It appeared there only twice on a substantial scale in all these years, in 1892–3 and in 1902–4, and then with relatively few fatalities. In that sense, therefore, the 'Leicester method' might perhaps be held to have justified itself in practice. At the same time it is worth noting that in 1903, during the last serious outbreak, there was a sudden recourse to vaccination again. When confronted with the disease itself, immediate and malignant, the people of Leicester turned back to the preventive that the medical profession, by an overwhelming majority, continued to trust.[1]

There was one other disease from which the town suffered to a quite exceptional extent: the 'summer diarrhoea' that particularly affected young children. The infant mortality of Leicester remained formidably high throughout the Victorian age, and beyond it. In 1859 more than half the total of deaths were of children under five; out of the 623 parochial districts of England and Wales there were only thirty others in which the figure was so high.[2] It was kept up by this virulent diarrhoea – which affected people of all ages severely: over 11 per cent of all deaths in Leicester in 1866–75 were due to it.

What was the cause, and what might be the cure? Plainly it was due in part to the town's generally insanitary condition, aggravated by the rapid increase of its population and the long delay in providing it with efficient sewerage. That did not seem, however, to be the whole explanation, and many attempts were made to investigate it further. In the 'seventies the infant mortality began to be attributed, by some intelligent observers, to the changing conditions of employment, the decline in domestic industry, the multiplication of factories, which drew married women away from their homes and from the care of their families. 'It is impossible for mothers engaged in factories to bring up their children properly ... As long

[1] This controversy is treated in brief in VCHL iv. 280–3; more fully but less well in 43 TLAS (1967–8) 35–44.
[2] RMOH 1859, 7–8.

therefore as outdoor female labour is required in Leicester for the various manufactories, the mortality that arises from improper feeding will continue.' That was the bluntly-expressed verdict of the Medical Officer of Health in 1878. He went on to urge the Corporation to assist the establishment of day nurseries, to look after the children of working mothers.[1] His diagnosis was by no means universally accepted. But it was in the Mid-Victorian age that the economic and social change he was speaking of advanced most notably; and the figures remained year after year much the same. The town was thoroughly drained, the supply of pure water grew abundant, and still the children died – nearly 300 annually in the 'nineties at less than a year old – from the same cause. When the change came at last, early in the new century, there was nothing specific to account for it: nothing more than the guess that it was a consequence of the accumulated progress in sanitary habits and nutrition that had then come over the town. In 1912 it could be noted, for the first time, that there was no visitation of the summer diarrhoea.[2]

Long before this the improvement in the town's health as a whole became very marked. The high general death rate that had characterised Leicester from about 1840 to 1870 had been decisively reduced. By 1874, at 23·3:1000, it could claim to be the lowest shown by any manufacturing town in England.[3] In 1900–9 it came down to 14·6:1000. Judged by this standard, in sixty years Leicester had changed from being one of the unhealthiest towns in England to become one of the healthiest.

A large contribution, inexpressible in figures, was certainly made to this improvement by the energetic development of medicine and nursing in the town. The Infirmary, having gone through a dreary civil war in 1854–60, when the governing body and the medical staff were not on speaking terms,[4] advanced strikingly in the value of its work and in the affection of those it served. It received a substantial legacy in 1860, which enabled it to undertake much-needed rebuilding and extension, so as to provide for a maximum of 200 patients. Further extensions came presently. A single ward was set aside for children in 1875, which grew into a separate wing for them in 1889; a new out-patients' department was opened in 1904.

The money required came in part from large donors, but also from a host of small subscribers, including a good many poor people. As early as 1823 we hear of a subscription of two guineas from the workmen in a factory. In 1873 the experiment of a Hospital Saturday was tried. It produced over £600 and at once became

---

[1] W. Johnston, *Borough of Leicester: Report on the Principal Zymotic Diseases during* 1877 [1878], 18. Cf. 28 RLDM 13, 30 *ibid.* 10.
[2] For references to the discussion of infant mortality see VCHL iv. 280.
[3] RMOH 1874, 3.
[4] Frizelle and Martin, *Leicester Royal Infirmary*, 110–13.

established as an annual event. Ten years later the proceeds had almost trebled; in 1903–4 they reached nearly £8,000. The income from this source added steadily to the revenues of the Infirmary. But Hospital Saturday did something more: it expressed the affection and gratitude felt by the working classes to an institution that helped them at many crises in their lives. It did something to make the Infirmary a corporate responsibility of the whole town.

These years of development brought great changes in the treatment of disease – the use of anaesthetics, antisepsis, innumerable improvements in the techniques of the physicians and surgeons. No less important, they brought a revolution in nursing. In the 1850s, although doubtless the Infirmary was served by some devoted and responsible women, it had its Betsy Prigs. In 1852 one of them was brought back, drunk, by a policeman. Of nurses in general, it was observed in 1860 that they were 'proverbially as cruel a set of women as are to be found in all England'.[1] None of those in the Leicester Infirmary was fully trained until 1862, when three were appointed from St Thomas's Hospital in London. Four years later an Institution for Trained Nurses was set up, to provide district nurses for the poor, as well as nurses to work for fees in private houses. Leicester was early in this field, preceded only by Liverpool, Manchester, London, and one or two other towns. In 1875 the Institution was strong enough to be entrusted with the provision of nurses for the Infirmary itself.[2] The whole working of the Infirmary depended on the steady supply of nurses, well selected and well trained; the Institution did much to ensure that they were forthcoming. The district nurses it provided were even more important, perhaps, to the general well-being of the town. Competent, unobtrusive, reliable, they played their part – perhaps, if it could be exactly analysed, a large part – in the improvement in the health of Leicester. How can one begin to estimate the comfort and relief that, over the last 100 years, they have dispensed?

5

The transformation of the town's physical condition, and of its citizens' health, coincided almost exactly in time with the transformation of its educational system.

In the 1860s that system was, in one leading respect, disgraceful. The old grammar school was dead. An effort had been made to re-found it, with the Town Council's assistance, in the 'fifties; but that had come to nothing.[3] Alderman

[1] Wilkie Collins, *The Woman in White* (Everyman edn), 193.
[2] Frizelle and Martin, 135–40; 22 RLDM 16, 23 *ibid.* 9; Ellis, *Records*, 93.
[3] G. Cowie, *History of Wyggeston's Hospital* (1893), 50–1.

Newton's School continued, moving from its first building in Holy Bones to a new one erected for it, close to St Martin's church, in 1864 (Plate 2b).[1] Of the two new schools established in the bustling, contentious 1830s (i.175), the Proprietory School had failed. The Collegiate, after a useful life, was now running into financial difficulties, and it too was shut down in 1866. Here then was a town of 90,000 people offering no public education, and not much private, that went beyond the three Rs.

The building of elementary schools by the religious denominations had proceeded fast. Twenty-three were opened between 1846 and 1870, providing some 3,000 additional places. At the end of that period accommodation was available, in some form, for about three-quarters of the town's children aged between three and thirteen. Only 56 per cent of those children, however, were actually in attendance.[2]

In education, then, the Early Victorian town had a mixed record. It showed energy in the provision of elementary schools, but it was less successful in getting the children into them. In education above the elementary level it did not progress at all; indeed it moved backwards.

The progress made had been due almost entirely to local initiative. In 1870 however a decisive change came, with the intervention of the State. The Act of that year provided for the establishment of School Boards, to build and maintain schools of their own, financed from the rates, working side by side with those supported by the denominational bodies. The Leicester School Board was set up in 1871. Its work did not get under way very quickly, hampered by acrid sectarian disputes.[3] But its first schools, in Syston Street and King Richards' Road were opened on 19 January 1874, followed in the course of that year by three more. By 1882 the Board was supplying places for slightly more children than the denominational schools; by 1903 for seven of the town's children out of ten. Its education was not provided free until 1891, save to those parents who could prove total inability to pay. Nor was it at first compulsory. This weakness was particularly important in Leicester, where young children were so extensively employed in industry; and even after compulsion had been introduced in 1880 a long battle lay ahead to secure the children's attendance at school. Very many parents were prosecuted for failing in this duty. They often hid the children at home and sent them off to work as soon as the inspector's back was turned.

In the long run it was children of this kind who owed most of all to the Act of 1870. The earlier efforts to educate them had been pitiful. A well-intentioned

[1] The history of the school from 1836 to 1914 is clearly told by I. A. W. Place in 30 TLAS (1960) 22–44.
[2] Figures in VCHL iv. 330.
[3] 33 TLAS (1957) 53.

Workshops Regulation Act came into force in 1868, compelling employers to provide education for the children who worked for them. Good employers complied. The rest either ignored it (many of the small shops were in back courts and alleys, difficult for prying investigators to penetrate) or dismissed all their children who came within its terms.[1] As Dare put it, from his intimate experience, in 1872:

> Numbers of little boys, especially in the shoe business, are drudging from five or six o'clock in the morning till eight or nine at night, amongst the *private* nailers and finishers. There is neither time nor inclination for evening instruction. They are overwrought, restless, inattentive, and many fall asleep.[2]

Liberal and individualist as he was in his outlook, he had been advocating that education should be made compulsory for twenty years past; he knew how much depended on the adoption of the principle and its rigid enforcement.[3]

A number of specialised schools, for the teaching of children unusually disadvantaged, and some new techniques, were brought into use at this time, in which Leicester experimented intelligently. As early as 1876 the Board began to consider setting up an Industrial School, to provide for children whose home life was so bad that it nullified their education. The idea was fulfilled in 1881, when a school on these lines was opened at Desford, which today has behind it a long record of admirable achievement. The Froebel methods of infant teaching were introduced early into the town, owing chiefly to the influence of Mrs William Evans (Dare's daughter), the first woman member of the School Board. The education of the deaf and dumb began in Leicester in 1885; School Boards were not obliged to provide it, in the country at large, until 1894.

Elementary education thus developed, in all its branches, a very long way in the last generation of the nineteenth century. The teaching of older children, so lamentably deficient in 1870, also made progress in these years, though more slowly and with less striking success. The Grammar School was at long last reconstituted under the Wyggeston Trustees. New buildings were erected for a boys' school, on the site of the old Hospital, and brought into use in 1877. In the following year a corresponding school was opened for girls.

There, in that last field, an effort was very much needed. Although there were a number of private girls' schools in the town, few of them had the merits of Belmont House (i.176). The majority were small and feeble. They touched the working classes scarcely at all. The impression they made on those whose parents could afford to pay their modest fees was not, as a rule, a happy one. The daughter of a vicar of St Margaret's thus recalled her education in the 1870s:

[1] 23 RLDM 6.
[2] 27 *ibid.* 13.
[3] 7 *ibid.* 6.

Occasionally, I was sent to a day school. If a woman lost her husband, or a rich man went bankrupt, the widows or daughters set up a school, with no further preparation, poverty their only certificate, and I was sent *pour encourager les autres*, as a girl's education did not matter. . . .

My sojourns however were always brief; for when my father found out some gross piece of ignorance, generally the mispronunciation of a classical word – we were taught to call Psyche *Fisk* and Melpomene as a tri-syllable – I was at once removed; a false quantity was to him an abomination.[1]

The new Wyggeston Schools were both given a good start, through the appointment of able heads. The Rev. James Went grew into an admired, almost a commanding, figure in the educational life of the community. Though he was a competent grammar-school headmaster of the orthodox kind, his ideas of education ranged considerably further. He realised, sooner than most men of his profession, the urgent need to improve technical education in England, and he provided instruction in evening classes at the school from 1884 onwards. Those classes were held in a new building, added to it at this time and given up largely to laboratories and workshops. Under his long reign (1877–1919), the re-founded school was brought into line with the best grammar schools of its sort, and kept there.[2]

His colleague, Miss Ellen Leicester, had served under Miss Buss at the North London Collegiate School for Girls, and was deeply imbued with its ideas. She presided over the girls' school from 1878 to 1902, when at the age of sixty-one (and without any prospect of a pension) she retired, in the conviction that it was time for a younger woman to take over.[3] Similar influences were potent elsewhere in Leicester, for Belmont House had passed in 1876 under the direction of Miss Anna Chrysogon Beale, sister of Dorothea Beale of Cheltenham. As a woman she was difficult, perhaps hardly lovable; but she set high standards in her school, and she too appreciated the importance of the teaching of science. There cannot have been many other private girls' schools in England about the year 1880 whose curriculum included biology.[4]

The teaching of science in the Leicester schools soon came to be reinforced rather unexpectedly. Alderman Newton's foundation had continued on its old path, not unsuccessful but in no way distinguished. His Trustees seem to have recognised that the school was growing out of date, and in 1884 they decided to

[1] M. W. Nevinson, *Life's Fitful Fever* (1926), 8.
[2] There is a full obituary of Canon Went in 36 *Wyggestonian* (1935–6) 46–50, and a fine portrait of him hangs in the school hall.
[3] Ellis, *Records*, 231–2.
[4] *Ibid.*, 261–5.

close it and to re-found it on new lines. The school was opened again in 1888. In advertising for a headmaster, the governors proclaimed the direction of their thinking: 'science (including practical chemistry) and drawing of special importance'. The first appointment they made did not prove notable, but the second headmaster of the new foundation, J. W. Muston, took the school far and fast along the road the governors had indicated. Too far and too fast perhaps. He developed the upper ranges of the school's work a long way beyond what was expected of a 'Public Elementary School', to a point where it began to compete seriously with the senior Wyggeston foundation. In November 1901 the Board of Education sent down two of its officers to investigate what was happening.

They strongly condemned everything they found, concluding that the recent development of the school had been wholly *ultra vires*, and that the governors were personally liable for the cost it had involved. The result might well have been more drastic than it was if the Government had not been carrying through a new Education Bill at the time, to deal especially with secondary education. It was clearly undesirable to allow a school that provided efficient teaching, however irregularly, to disappear. After protracted negotiations agreement was reached in 1907–9, under which the school was taken over by the municipality. Throughout all this commotion Muston remained headmaster, and the scientific bent of the school continued until after he retired in 1923. By that time, it may be added, the school was no longer denominational, except that the small number of scholarships at the disposal of the governors were confined to Anglican boys. If Alderman Newton had revisited Leicester 150 years after his death, he would have found his school unrecognisably different from what he had intended; and being choleric, no doubt he would have voiced his disapproval. But he ought to have been proud of it at heart.[1]

The science teaching introduced into the Leicester schools in the later Victorian age was thought of primarily in vocational terms. Vocational training was by no means new in the town: the Mechanics' Institute had attempted to provide it in the 1830s. But that effort had failed, and nothing was developed, to a systematic plan, to take its place until 1870. A group of Leicester business men then initiated a School of Art, with a strictly utilitarian objective: to raise the standard of industrial and commercial design. That this School was, at its inception, a private venture reflects no discredit on the Corporation. Nothing would have empowered it to make the School an annual grant. Nor were the School Boards, when they were formed, allowed to touch any kind of further education. There was, however, one source of public money that soon became available to the new School. Grants to assist such work could be made from funds at the disposal of the Science and Art Department at South Kensington.

[1] For the whole of this story cf. 36 TLAS (1960) 38–43.

The School of Art was established first in a converted warehouse in Pockling-ton's Walk. In 1877 it moved into accommodation designed for it in an extension to the Museum, paid for by the Town Council and by private subscription in roughly equal parts.[1] The Council remained inhibited from supporting the School of Art with any annual payment until the passing of the Technical Instruction Act of 1889, aided by the timely arrival of 'whisky money' in 1890.[2] It established a Technical Education Committee in 1892, which was a sign of its developing interest in this field. Thenceforward it began, to a fast-increasing extent, to look on the School of Art as its own.

At the same time the Council became closely involved in technical education of other kinds as well. It had had no hand in the provision of evening classes made at the Wyggeston Boys' School in 1884. They too owed their origin to private initiative, from the Chamber of Commerce, which began to interest itself in the matter in 1881.[3] But their value soon came to be appreciated, and the Council recognised that in much the same way as it had recognised the value of the School of Art. There was nothing to stop it from spending money on providing accom-modation, and in 1892 it took the first step towards erecting permanent buildings to house the Technical School, with the Art School joined to it. It bought two houses on the west side of the Newarke enclosure (occupying part of the site of the vanished collegiate church), and then proceeded to build in their ample gardens. The result was an impressive pile, designed by the leading Leicester architect of the time, Samuel Perkins Pick, which was brought into use in 1897. In the year before the First World War began, the two Schools together had about 100 full-time students and 1,200 part-time. In addition, the Local Education Authority was providing for about 850 students in technical and commercial courses.[4]

The municipality, having taken over these Schools, supported them well. It may have done so with the more energy and pleasure from an uneasy sense that the town's record in secondary education had not been happy. Here was a chance to start something new, and to keep well up in the march of progress. The town took it, and came to feel a proprietorship and a pride in the result.

These two institutions did not supply all the education, outside the schools, that was offered in Leicester. Side by side with them, and originating further back in time, were a number of private ventures. Some of these were adult schools con-

---

[1] Storey, 34–5.

[2] For the history of 'whisky money' see R. C. K. Ensor, *England, 1870–1914* (1936), 204n.

[3] 22 *Report* 8.

[4] VCHL iii. 260–1. The Chamber of Commerce gave the venture continuous attention and support. Cf. the conference it called on the matter in 1902, fully recorded in 42 *Report* 26–62.

nected with religious bodies – the Unitarians and the Quakers were pioneers here; the counterpart of the denominational schools for children. One remarkable enterprise of this kind depended entirely on a single woman, Mary Royce, who carried it on, first in Sanvey Gate and then in Church Gate, from 1868 to her death in 1892.

But all these efforts, valuable as they were and highly appreciated by many of those they helped, were overshadowed by one that they would have agreed in acknowledging as pre-eminent: the Working Men's College established in 1862.[1] The credit for this belongs to the vicar of St Martin's, the Rev. D. J. Vaughan, whose name the College eventually came to bear. Vaughan was much influenced, through his friend John Llewellyn Davies, by F. D. Maurice's ideas of the education of working men. He had observed them in Maurice's Working Men's College at first hand when he succeeded Davies in the charge of a Whitechapel parish in 1858. From there he moved to Leicester in 1860. When he arrived, the Mechanics' Institute was dying on its feet. The general opinion among educated people interested in such things was that no venture of the kind could succeed, at least for the present, in the town. That view was expressed very clearly in the discussion at the Literary and Philosophical Society in 1862 on a paper by Maurice entitled 'Working Men's Colleges'. Vaughan rejected such pessimism, and very shortly afterwards he established a 'Reading Room and Library for Working Men' in his parish, which that autumn began to offer evening classes.

What was thus done in Leicester under Vaughan's guidance was also done in a number of other towns, such as Liverpool, Manchester, Sheffield, and Wolverhampton. But few of these institutions had any long or flourishing life. The one in Manchester was absorbed by Owens College; the rest, before very long, languished. In Leicester, on the other hand, Vaughan's foundation – which changed its title to 'Working Men's College' in 1868 – went on, to play an energetic part, well sustained, in the Late Victorian town.

In its early years the College's chief service was to provide the rudiments of education for those who had failed to secure them when they were children. With the kind of men who took advantage of its opportunities, that failure had been due not to laziness or stupidity but to the conditions of their employment and to the shortcomings of the educational provision that the town afforded. In this respect the College, and the adult schools, offered something that was of peculiar importance to the generation who were already grown up when the Act of 1870 was passed and were stimulated by it to seek whatever educational chances were open to them. These men continued for some time to constitute the basis of the College's work. The fees it charged were kept as low as possible, with them in mind; and

[1] For all that follows on this subject see Professor A. J. Allaway's two accounts, in 33 TLAS (1957) 45–58 and in his *Vaughan College Leicester, 1862–1962* (1962).

yet, even so, in 1878–9 when trade was depressed attendance fell, partly because working men found themselves unable to afford even those fees, partly from 'the anxiety of mind and the loss of spirit produced by the prospect before them'.

Quite early, however, in the College's history it began to see its duties in wider terms. In 1877 we read of an 'endeavour to extend the advantages of the College . . . upwards . . . in the social scale, by opening classes for young men engaged in business'. The institution soon extended its range far beyond the horizons of the adult schools. St John's Ambulance classes were provided; there was instruction in shorthand (with the lure of 'Mr Pitman's certificates'), and in typewriting from 1892. In the 'eighties the teaching of science grew more advanced. There was talk of electric lighting in the town; at once we see a class in electricity springing up. The College began to provide classes for women in 1881. They remained separate from those for men, however; mixed classes did not appear until 1909. At a higher academic level University Extension classes had established themselves – Leicester, Nottingham, and Derby were the first three towns in which they were provided, from Cambridge; and, though an early attempt to graft the two together failed, the College saw it as one of its functions to prepare students for Extension classes. In some people's minds there was now a bolder ambition. In Nottingham the Extension Movement had led to the establishment of a University College, which began work in 1881. Why should not the same thing happen in Leicester? In 1877 the *Chronicle* referred to Vaughan's College as 'this important local industrial university'; in 1888 the same paper was speaking of its chances to grow into a rival of the College at Nottingham. Those ideas were too grandiose. Nottingham had important things that Leicester lacked: large-scale private generosity, enthusiasm among at least a few members of the Town Council. But the *Chronicle* was not alone in voicing the aspiration. It appears too, repeatedly, in the Literary and Philosophical Society's discussions.[1] It was not to be realised until the next century, but Vaughan's College paved the way towards it, and in the meantime it notably broadened the educational opportunities and the outlook of the town. By 1900 men who owed much of their education to it – Jabez Chaplin, for instance, and T. W. Walker – were being elected to the Town Council. They were not unmindful of their debt in the years to come.

6

Leicester had done itself credit by the early establishment of its Museum. True, the institution was run on a shoe-string, and it was both dingy and overcrowded with an incoherent display of exhibits; but in those respects it was like nearly all

[1] J. Simmons, *New University* (1958), 57–8.

museums in the provinces at that time, in this country and on the Continent. A twentieth-century Liberal, looking back to his childhood in Leicester in the 'sixties, dismissed it with contempt as 'a pitiful Museum of stuffed birds and Roman "remains"'.[1] All the money found for it from the rates was expended on administration and on paying off by instalments the purchase price of its building. The Literary and Philosophical Society contributed £52 10s. a year towards the salary of the Curator and about £50 towards buying specimens. That represented the whole of the Museum's purchase fund. For the rest, it was dependent on the generosity of its well-wishers. In the Mid-Victorian age the Museum became the natural depository for the antiquities that were turned up in the course of excavations for the new streets and the sewers then being built so rapidly. Especial attention was paid to objects of the Roman period, and the material thus assembled forms a valuable element in the collections of the Department of Antiquities today. The Curator, J. E. Weatherhead, watched conscientiously the building-work that was going forward in the town, and when he spoke of the finds that had been made he commanded respect.[2] He was an able man, who was not well treated in Leicester.[3] For the rest, the Museum devoted itself chiefly to botany and zoology. The commendable *Handbook* that it issued, in nine parts, in 1864–9 treats of natural history alone.

What that Liberal critic failed to appreciate was the striking fact that the Museum existed at all, and the potential it offered for the future. It was a substructure, on which something big and useful could be built. Drab though it might appear, it created its own loyalties, an affectionate tradition that brought it powerful support in later years.

The town had few other cultural institutions of which it could be proud. The Literary and Philosophical Society, which had fathered the Museum, continued its steady good work. Looking back to the subjects of its meetings in these years, one must be struck by their almost uniform seriousness, and much of the discussion was evidently jejune. But at least the Society kept going, and it provided a useful forum of debate on important matters of the time: either matters of current controversy or projects for the future – like the establishment of a free public library.[4] In the 'nineties it initiated the plan for the publication in the borough records, and so put every student of the town's history in its debt.

In some other towns this was a role filled, and more effectively filled, by the press. Leicester had respectable weekly newspapers, in the Conservative *Journal*

---

[1] H. W. Nevinson, *Changes and Chances* (1923), 1.
[2] 2 TLAS (1870) 301–2; 3 *ibid.* (1874) 112–15.
[3] 54 *Transactions of the Leicester Literary and Philosophical Society* (1960) 9.
[4] Cf. *ibid.*, 1835–79, 178, 230, 282, 290.

and the Liberal *Chronicle and Mercury*. In 1872 they were joined by the Liberal *Daily Post*, a morning paper, and that in its turn found a rival in the *Daily Mercury* (published in the afternoon) two years later. These papers all had their merits; the student of Victorian Leicester today may well regard them with admiration. James Thompson, the editor of the *Chronicle*, was an invaluable citizen,[1] who immersed himself in the town's history and did much to preserve its antiquities. But none of these papers threw up a big man as editor, who became a leading force in moulding the thought of the community, like the Baines, father and son, in Leeds or C. P. Scott in Manchester – or even, to take an example from a smaller place, like Thomas Latimer in Exeter. There was something inimical in the very spirit of Leicester to the emergence of strength of that kind. Ideas tended to express themselves there more in corporate terms, through the Council, the religious bodies, the Literary and Philosophical Society.

The Leicestershire Archaeological Society, which was founded in 1855, quickly made some mark within its chosen field.[2] It was very much, as its title implied, a county society; but its headquarters were in the town, most of its meetings were held there, and the town provided its fair share of the most effective members, like James Thompson and Thomas North. Its strong county element became a useful asset, helping to keep town and county in some measure together when towards the close of the century, for political and economic reasons, they were drawing further apart.

As the Society grew, and slowly acquired respect, it became the principal defender of the remaining antiquities of Leicester, a watchdog against their destruction or ignorant and needless alteration. Much of its energy was devoted to discussing the restoration of churches. The Society is to be seen, for example, leaping into the controversy that surrounded Brandon's rebuilding of the spire of St Martin's in the 'sixties – finally coming down on the right side to recognise it for what it is, 'the finest steeple in Leicester'.[3] It tried hard to preserve Wyggeston's Hospital from destruction over a long course of years from 1863 to 1875 (Plate 2a). Here it had a good proposal for an alternative use for the building. The Society urged that the Hospital should be preserved and adapted to form part of the new school that the Trustees were seeking to found. That this reasonable argument did not prevail was due in part to the Town Council's anxiety to widen Peacock Lane – perhaps as much as to the Trustees' resolve to erect wholly new

---

[1] Politically, he was a pillar of moderate Liberalism; but in his early life he had been a very active Radical, even for a time a sub-editor of the Chartist *Northern Star*: PP 1852–3, xiv, QQ. 5829–35.

[2] For its history see *The Leicestershire Archaeological Society, 1855–1955* (1955).

[3] 45 TLAS (1970–1) 62–5.

accommodation.[1] We can still hear the ringing cry of Thomas North, when all was over and the buildings had been destroyed in 1875: 'What will the Trustees get in place of the old Hospital? ... A proposed modern gymnasium, at a considerable cost, and ninety-two pounds!!'[2] Later the Society was to fight another battle, of the same kind but much more important; and there it came out victorious (p. 56).

The natural concomitant and support of bodies like these was a good library. Leicester had had one of the earliest public libraries in any English town (i.81–2); and when, with changing intellectual and social habits, that library fell into disuse it might have been expected that its place would be taken by another. That happened to only a very limited extent. Private subscription libraries were established. The Leicester Permanent Library was set up in 1791, and after a chequered history was transferred in 1839 to the General News Room. But that was only for the well-to-do: the subscription was £1 5s. a year.[3] Otherwise, there was the Mechanics' Institute, which had a respectable library of its own but enjoyed only a short life. By 1860, for different reasons, both the Permanent Library and the Mechanics' Institute were in trouble. Neither could give the town the facilities that its people might reasonably expect. The new stirrings in education in the succeeding decade – especially in the education of adults – accentuated the need.

Responding to it, the Council resolved to set up a Free Library, to be paid for from the rates, in 1862. But that was a resolution, no more. Nothing was done to implement it. At this point one can almost listen in to 'the immovable incuriosity of the small municipal mind'.[4] The Council's inaction found sharp critics. 'How many towns are there in Great Britain of the size of Leicester without a Free Public Library?' cried one of them in 1868.[5] Nevertheless, the resolution of 1862 might have remained a dead letter for years if it had not been for one man, and one opportunity. The man was George Stevenson, son of a Baptist minister at Loughborough, a member of the Leicester Town Council since 1858 and Mayor in 1869–70. He had campaigned tirelessly for the provision of a Public Library and he won his reward when, in May 1869, the Council decided to carry out its decision of 1862. It was enabled to do so with effect and a nice economy because the Mechanics' Institute, which had been dying for some years, dropped dead in

[1] 2 ibid. (1870) 200, 206, 284; 4 ibid. (1878) 52, 105, 112, 229, 322, 237.
[2] 5 ibid. (1882) 13; Cowie, History of Wyggeston's Hospital, 68.
[3] F. S. Herne, History of the Town Library (1891: LRLP, vol. 9), 21–2, 25–7.
[4] The phrase is G. M. Young's: Victorian England (1955 edn.), 57.
[5] J. A. Picton, The Leicester Carnival (1868: LRLP, vol. 66), 12n. It is fair to Leicester to note that the ratepayers of Hull decided twice, in 1857 and 1872, not to have any such library: J. Mayhall, Annals of Yorkshire (n.d.), iii. 455.

1870. The Council then acquired the New Hall that the Institute had occupied (the Central Lending Library today) at a knockdown price of a little over £3000, and it received as a gift the Institute's library. Even those Councillors who continued to think a Public Library an unwarranted extravagance must have rejoiced in the bargain. On this basis a reading room was opened on 9 January 1871; the Lending and Reference Departments began work three months later.

The Library was supported out of the proceeds of a halfpenny rate. This income (about £450 a year) enabled it to pay a Librarian and a minute staff and to keep the building lighted and warmed. It provided little for the purchase of books. Additions to the original stock came chiefly from gifts. Stevenson himself gave long runs of the serious periodicals. Samuel Stone, the Town Clerk (whose powerful support had done much to help the establishment of the Library), added works by the standard novelists, and when he died in 1873 he left it £50. Other legacies and gifts came later: from Charles Clifton, a Leicester man who had emigrated to the United States; from the Radical politician P. A. Taylor, one of the M.P.s for the borough for more than twenty years – over 1,600 volumes were received from him between 1874 and 1885. In 1883 the first branch library was opened, in Garendon Street, in a building paid for by a generous Councillor, Israel Hart, who also gave 1,500 books towards its stock.

Such private benefactions enabled the Council to keep down its expenditure on the Library. Not solely from parsimony: these were years of very heavy expenditure on sanitary improvement. In 1885–6 the rate was raised, partly to enable the Library to accumulate funds for the opening of further branches – a clear sign that the demand for its services was growing. By the end of the century there were six.

It is not a simple story of progress, slow but unchecked. The first Librarian had to be dismissed after an audit had been held.[1] When the Committee decided in 1891 to open the Library experimentally on Sunday evenings, Stevenson, who had been its Chairman for twenty years, resigned in protest.[2] In the next year the Committee ran into trouble through its decision that the racing and betting news must be obliterated from the daily papers the Library supplied. It expressed its firm conviction that 'to diminish the facilities for folly must have some effect in diminishing the practice of it. The public reading room was becoming a recognised school for teaching boys to bet'. This rule was enforced for over twenty years.[3] As the century closed the original building grew seriously overcrowded. It became necessary to stop adding any books to the reference section because there was no room for them, and its plight was reflected in a serious falling-off in the number

[1] 17 *Report of the Libraries Committee* 6.
[2] 20 *ibid.* 5.
[3] 21 *ibid.* 6; 42 *ibid.* 5.

1. The tower of the Town Hall (F. J. Hames, 1876). In the foreground part of the fountain, designed by the same architect.

2a. Wyggeston's Hospital: front of the chapel facing Peacock Lane. Demolished 1875 (cf. p. 30).

2b. Alderman Newton's School (1864): photograph taken in 1867 from the new steeple of St Martin's church.

3. St Peter's church, in the Highfields (architect, G. E. Street; built 1874–9).
Photograph taken 1968, before the destruction of the spire.

4. West Bridge Mills (William Flint, *c.* 1848). Now occupied by Messrs Pex Ltd.

5a. North Bridge Mills. In the foreground, Slater Street Board School, one of the first to be erected (1874).

5b. Britannia Works, Granby Street (corner of Calais Hill). Demolished 1962.

Messrs. Preston & Son, Southgate Street.

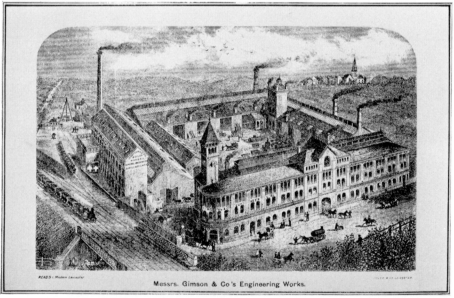

Messrs. Gimson & Co's Engineering Works.

6. Two commercial buildings as depicted in Read: (a) Preston's boot factory, Southgate Street and Bakehouse Lane. (b) Gimson's Vulcan Engineering Works (cf. p. 5).

7a. National Provincial (now National Westminster) Bank (William Millican, 1869). On the site of the Three Crowns Inn, at the corner of Granby Street and Horsefair Street.

7b. Westminster (now National Westminster) Bank. Architect, S. Perkins Pick, 1902.

8. Late Victorian street scenes: (a) The Newarke, *c.* 1895, shortly before the building of the Technical College, in the garden to the left. (b) Road works, corner of Fosse Road and Noble Street.

9a. Stonesby House, De Montfort Square: built for F. J. Morley of the firm of Richard Morley & Sons, 1869. Architect James Morley. Subsequently Toc H, Mark XI.

9b. Nos. 169–85 Narborough Road (1886–90).

10a. Panels from the offices of Thos. Cook & Sons Ltd., erected 1894 (architect, W. A. Catlow) as a memorial to Cook himself (cf. i. 157). The four panels stand side by side on the building; they depict transport developments in the first 50 years of the firm's life.

10b. East Gates Coffee House (Edward Burgess, 1885): still extant, serving very different purposes.

11a. The High Street: photograph taken shortly before its complete reconstruction from 1902 onwards. The tall building on the left was the sole surviving fragment of Lord's Place, the town house of the Earls of Huntingdon (see i. 63, 96).

11b. De Montfort Hall (Stockdale Harrison, 1913; cf. pp. 50–1).

SIR THOMAS!

Mrs. Victoria.—Well climbed, Tommy. You shall have a bun. You deserve it.

12. Sir Thomas Wright (cf. pp. 121–2). Cartoon by W. J. Urquhart: *The Wyvern*, 9 June 1893.

13. Leaders of the march of the unemployed from Leicester to London, 1905 (cf. p. 59): left to right, George White, Rev. F. L. Donaldson, Amos Sherriff.

15. War Memorial (Sir Edwin Lutyens, 1925; cf. pp. 70–1).

14. Two pieces of *art nouveau*: (a) Wholesale Market – arch of the main S. entrance (architect: Walter Brand). Demolished 1972. (b) Cabinet and stand, in ebony inlaid with mother of pearl, designed by Ernest Gimson and made at the Daneway Workshops 1908. Height 3ft 10½in. Now in Leicester Museums collection.

16a. The Clock Tower in its original setting. Note (left to right) St Mark's spire, the horse tram, the hansom cab, and the shop of John Burton, to whose initiative the erection of the Tower was chiefly due (pp. 48–9).

16b. The Clock Tower, 1973. Littlewood's store on the right.

of those who used it. In 1899 the Committee said roundly that the accommodation was 'little short of a disgrace'.[1]

Plans for a new Library were prepared; but they were not realised until, in Leicester as in so many other towns, Andrew Carnegie munificently agreed to bear the greater part of the cost. On 8 May 1905 he opened the new building, which adjoined the Town Hall. Designed by Edward Burgess, it was well up to the standards of its time. By then the stock of books was seven times as large as it had been at the outset.

George Stevenson, to whom the Libraries owed most, had died at the age of eighty-four in the previous year. Public bodies are seldom felicitous in their tributes on such occasions. But the Libraries Committee got it admirably right: 'His name deserves to be bracketed with those of Wyggeston and Newton, as the local heroes of education'.[2] It noted with satisfaction that his portrait, subscribed for at the time of his retirement, hung in the reading room. It survives today, but unseen in an attic.

Much had been done, through public and private action, to equip the town with the libraries it needed. But as far as the Council was concerned, one can never feel that it was done *con amore*. Again and again its policy was contrasted unfavourably with that of other large towns. 'Leicester is the only town of importance that does not allow to the Library a full penny rate', observed the Committee in 1911.[3] In this cultural provision Leicester never recovered its tardy and grudging start.

7

The religious life of the town took on a richer diversity in the later Victorian age. The thirty-five churches and chapels of 1851 grew to eighty-six in 1900. The number would have been larger if it had not been for the closing of a fair number of Dissenting chapels. At least sixteen belonging to the Baptists and Wesleyans alone fell out of use during the Victorian age.[4] In some cases this was because they had given way to bigger buildings elsewhere, but the figure indicates quite truly the transient nature of many of the congregations, which rose or fell or removed themselves according to the liking they felt for their pastors and the doctrines they preached. The Anglican church grew more steadily, being little subject – in the nineteenth century, at any rate – to upheavals of this kind; but it could hardly feel, any more than the Dissenting bodies, that its expansion was keeping pace with the

[1] 28 *ibid*. 6.
[2] 33 *ibid*. 6. See the obituary of Stevenson in *Leicester Chronicle*, 30 January 1904.
[3] 40 *Report of the Libraries Committee* 6.
[4] VCHL iv. 391–3.

growth of the town, still less that it was overtaking the accumulated arrears of the past. The Roman Catholics remained a small community, as they had always been in Leicester. Their first mass centre, in a house in Causeway Lane, had given place to the church of Holy Cross in 1819. They opened three other churches in 1853–96.[1]

There is little to be heard in Leicester of the extremes of belief that unsettled so many more volatile communities. The Mormons won some success in the town in the 1840s, persuading a number of converts to make the arduous journey over the Atlantic and the American continent to their Eden in the far west. Joseph Dare occasionally notes the activities of wild revivalists: the Fire Brigade of Jesus, for example, which rampaged through Leicester for a brief moment in 1865.[2] (He also records the survival of primitive superstition, pagan in its origin: like the long-established trust in the healing powers of Amelia Woodcock,[3] the Wise Woman whom the afflicted went out to visit at Wing in Rutland.) Small sects multiplied in obscurity, often enjoying only a short life, but sometimes doggedly tenacious, to survive into our own time.

Within the Established Church there was occasional trouble over ritualistic practices. Of the ancient parishes, only St Margaret's tended in that direction. But some of the newer churches established themselves under a strong Tractarian influence: St Andrew's, for example, and most notably St Paul's, in the Westcotes district. Its first Vicar, the Rev. James Mason, was the outstanding Anglo-Catholic of Leicester, and he encountered much opposition from troubled and noisy Protestants in the 'seventies. It is a tribute to his remarkable personality that he won through, to achieve in his forty years' incumbency (1871–1911) a real eminence in the town. In the lock-out in the boot and shoe manufacture of 1895, workers and employers accepted him as an arbitrator. In the last small-pox epidemic in 1904 he ministered with heroic and tireless fortitude. Striding along in his cassock, he was a tremendous figure – 6 ft. 3 in. tall, his beard luxuriant and untrimmed; a presence of a sort seldom felt in Leicester.[4] That the town should have come, first to accept and then to admire a man so profoundly alien to all its traditions, is one more demonstration of its deep-seated tolerance.

At the opposite pole of spiritual experience stood the Secularists, who entrenched themselves securely in Leicester in these years. They first appear in the early 'fifties, forming a Secular Society to pursue a 'philosophy of life which ignores

[1] *Ibid.*, ii. 62, 71. A manuscript of the register of the first Roman Catholic church is in BM Add. MS. 32632.
[2] 20 RLDM 7.
[3] 7 *ibid.* 10. Cf. 5 (5th series) *Notes and Queries* (1876) 4–5, 375.
[4] Cf. J. E. Hextall and A. L. Brightman, *Fifty Years . . . at St Paul's Leicester* (1921).

theology', but their history is discontinuous until 1867.[1] The Society owed much to the support of one man: Josiah Gimson, who was just beginning to make a special position for himself in the development of engineering in the town. Under him, a subscription was set on foot for the building of a Secular Hall. A company was formed, which bought 2000 sq. yds of land in Humberstone Gate, at a price of £4,500, and after a long financial struggle the Hall was opened in 1881. It survives (facing Sainsbury's) today, still bearing terracotta busts of Socrates, Jesus, Voltaire, Tom Paine, and Robert Owen – selected on the ground that they stood 'in a general way for wholesome criticism, for revolt against priestly pretensions, and for endeavours after a happier social environment'. Mrs Besant, Bradlaugh, and G. J. Holyoake were present at the Hall's opening. In later years William Morris spoke there, Hyndman and the Fabians, Bernard Shaw and H. G. Wells. Its Sunday meetings continue uninterruptedly still.

The Leicester Secularists set out rather to question religion than to destroy it. That was certainly the spirit Josiah Gimson and his son Sydney (Quakers in their background) sought to foster. Their social activities were genuinely important to them, in many ways scarcely distinguishable from those of the Nonconformists. But not in all. They were, as we should expect, vehement anti-Sabbatarians; and in 1885 a great commotion was caused by the determination of the Secular Cricket Club to play on Sundays. The games were broken up by rowdies, the police refused to intervene, denunciations thundered from pulpits, and in the end the attempt had to be abandoned.[2] The Secularists did indeed stir up antagonism: even moderate Anglicans like D. J. Vaughan attacked them long and fiercely. But they too held on, quietly victorious in the end, as they must have considered themselves, over 'priestly pretensions'. Rejecting religion, yet subscribing to an ethical code that was entirely Christian – they added another ingredient, a new spice, to the varieties of religious experience in Leicester.

8

Such were some of the intellectual recreations and spiritual activities of the town. What of its more popular amusements? In these years they changed notably. Perhaps this change can be epitomised by saying that whilst in 1880 cock-fighting was not extinct, and there was a rat-pit in Soar Lane 'patronised by dog fanciers from the nobleman down to the nailer', in 1904 the Leicester Fosse Club was receiving £600 for the transfer of its goalkeeper to Manchester City.[3]

[1] See F. J. Gould, *History of the Leicester Secular Society* (1900).
[2] Cf. *Annual Register*, 1885, 38.
[3] Read, 196, 286; VCHL iii. 289.

The pre-eminent historic sport in Leicester was horse-racing, though its social character had now become quite different. Instead of the eighteenth-century meetings, graced by the presence of the Leicestershire aristocracy and patronised by the Corporation, the Victorian races were a wholly popular affair. A substantial Gothic grand-stand was built for them in the 'sixties on the Victoria Park,[1] where the races continued to be held until they were transferred to the present course at Oadby in 1880. Meetings began to take place then several times a year, not in September alone. But it was to more professional standards, under increasingly rigid rules. The old happy-go-lucky spirit was less evident. The change also removed the one social occasion in the year that had always brought town and county together.[2]

There, to a limited extent, its place was taken by cricket. The origins of the game in Leicestershire go back into the eighteenth century; its development may have owed something to the hunting men who established themselves in the county so notably from about 1760 onwards.[3] In Leicester itself the game is first heard of in 1780. By 1824 the town could send a team to Sheffield, and win by one run. Next year a cricket ground was opened in Wharf Street. It was ten acres in extent and acquired a high reputation, far beyond Leicestershire. Matches of national interest were played there, between North and South, between Midland Counties or Northern Counties and the M.C.C. Twenty-two of Leicestershire would sometimes play an eleven of All England; at least twice, in 1856 and 1860, they won.

But the glory of Wharf Street (the only glory of any kind the street has known) came to an end after that last match, for in the following November the ground was sold for building. No substitute was immediately available. More of the important matches were played outside, in the county; those in Leicester took place on Victoria Park. The recovery from this setback was due to the Leicestershire Cricket Association, formed in 1873, and to a private company that bought twelve acres in the northern part of the parish of Aylestone and laid out a new ground there on Grace Road. In the very first season in 1878 the Australians came down. This was an innovation: Leicestershire was the first county to invite them. It even succeeded in defeating them in a subsequent match, in 1888. In 1895 Leicestershire became a first-class county. A new ground was opened on the Aylestone Road in 1901. These were the finest days of Leicestershire cricket, when the county scored 380 for the first wicket against Warwickshire in 1906,

[1] It seems to have acquired that name about 1865: 21 RLDM 3.

[2] Unaccountably, horse racing is hardly mentioned in VCHL.

[3] What follows is based on Mr E. E. Snow's two accounts, in his *History of Leicestershire Cricket* (1949) and in VCHL iii. 282–6.

and when one of the pair who made that stand, C. J. B. Wood, could carry his bat through both innings against Yorkshire.

In these years cricket attained its brief pre-eminence among the public sports of England. Neither of the two Aylestone grounds had quite the same national repute as their predecessor in Wharf Street. In this more sophisticated world, the primacy in the East Midlands passed to Trent Bridge at Nottingham. But Leicester was an important centre of the game, which gave a quiet and deep enjoyment to many thousands of people, its own citizens and those it drew in from outside.

The two football games were no less popular in winter, and in one of these too Leicester attained high estimation.[1] The first clubs in the town date from 1869. They were small and undistinguished. In 1880 they united in one Leicester Football Club, which organised rugby and association matches, more or less alternately. They were played on a ground in the Belgrave Road, and on Victoria Park. In 1884 the two games split apart, when the Leicester Fosse Club was formed to pursue soccer alone. In 1891–2 both clubs secured permanent grounds, the Fosse on Filbert Street, the Football Club ('The Tigers', from a change in their colours in 1888) on the Welford Road.

The Tigers made the more spectacular progress. Their new ground soon established itself as one of the best rugby grounds in England (it claimed to be second to Twickenham alone), and international matches were occasionally played there from 1902. The Tigers won the Midland Counties Cup twelve times in 1898–1913. In 1909 they played their first Christmas match against the Barbarians. That established itself as an annual event, which is still marked indelibly in the Leicester calendar.

The Fosse Club did not achieve the same distinction. It began to play in the second division of the Football League in 1894, shot into the first division in 1908–9, and then relapsed. Professionalism entered early into the game, when Harry Webb was brought over from Stafford Rangers in 1888; his inducement was 2s. 6d. a week. Here was the factor that perhaps did most to differentiate the character of the two clubs. The Fosse Club needed money, and soon big money, for professional fees, and it depended on the support of rich and influential citizens. Among its early Presidents was Sir Thomas Wright (see pp. 120–1). When it moved to Filbert Street, the rent was at first guaranteed by a leading draper in the town, Joseph Johnson. But his part in the matter was not merely external: four of his sons played, first and last, for the club. In financial terms, things came perhaps more easily to the Tigers, who were able to effect substantial improvements to their ground in 1909 and 1914. A good deal of their success, however, must also be ascribed to the energy and enthusiasm of their Hon. Secretary, Tom Crumbie, a famous figure who served the club with devotion from 1895 to 1928.

[1] Cf. *ibid.*, iii. 286–9.

These are the years in which organised sport, the team game, emerges, to become a leading element in the spare-time activities of England as a whole. It played a particularly important part in the life of Leicester. Few towns of its size could offer so wide a range of sports, of good quality, throughout the year. A number of forces combined to make that possible, and some were accidental, or external to the town: its geographical position and good railway communications, the county's pre-eminence in fox-hunting, the personal influence of men like Tom Crumbie or Sir Arthur Hazlerigg, the genial captain of the county cricket team from 1907. But these endeavours depended, in the end, on the support they received from the people of Leicester itself. Though that could vary disconcertingly, it was on the whole gratifying. Before the Mid-Victorian age the great majority of the townspeople had been absorbed in the weary struggle to get employment and keep it. Many of them needed to work overtime, when opportunity offered, in order to earn a wage even barely adequate to maintain their families. From 1860 onwards conditions began to change, with the shortening of hours, fuller and more various employment, a lightening of the physical labour of work through increased mechanisation. Gradually the people of Leicester began to be able to look about them and think what to do with their leisure. Some, as we have seen, put it into serious intellectual pursuits. Some chose to play team games or — by the turn of the century, more and more — to watch them. But these were not the only opportunities that were open now, to men and women with some time to spare, and a few coins to chink together.

There were other quiet sports and recreations that grew in popularity in these years. Some of them were immemorially old: walking out into the open country, for example, so much quicker and easier then. This simple pleasure came sometimes to be harnessed to self-improvement, as in Vaughan's College, when he led a party of teachers and students out to Kirby Muxloe Castle in 1866.[1] The favourite excursion was always to Bradgate Park, which the Greys generously opened to the public (though in 1864 they closed it for six days out of seven on account of hooligans).[2] Bathing in the river continued at all times, in spite of the serious objections to it; but swimming as a sport could hardly be fostered until the first Baths became available, in 1879.

The earliest of the town's new parks, the Abbey Park, was an admirable by-product of flood prevention. The undertaking was bitterly criticised and contested.[3] The cost of it was certainly high, in the scale of Victorian public expenditure. The bill for buying the Abbey Meadow seems to have come to about

[1] Allaway, *Vaughan College*, 5. Cf. 11 RLDM 13.
[2] 19 *ibid.* 8.
[3] Cf. Read, 24–5; 42 *Builder* (1882) 669–70.

£27,000;[1] by an Act of 1878 the Corporation was authorised to borrow another £25,000 for laying out sixty-six acres (but not the whole) of the Meadow as a park, providing it with the necessary buildings, and constructing the new Abbey Park Road. The total cost must therefore have approached £50,000 – at a time when the rate income of the Corporation averaged about £24,000 a year. But if one gives the critics a fair hearing, one must surely end by applauding the Corporation. The town was expanding northward in these years very fast, along the axis of the Belgrave Road, in close-packed streets, without trees, airless in summer, designed with the overriding purpose of accommodating the largest possible number of people in the smallest decent space. Unless they walked a mile or two – to the top of Mowmacre Hill, for instance – their only lung was the river bank; and that was a very unhealthy lung indeed. As for beauty, the chance to look at flowers or shrubs or well-grown trees, there was little enough of that. The Belgrave Road streets were healthier than those round Wharf Street and in the Old Town, occupied by previous generations. But they were dingy, even when new, and could give no lift at all to the spirit. The Abbey Park could, and did. In the scale of Mid-Victorian public improvements it must rank very high.

Shortly afterwards it was followed by another park on the opposite side of the town, at Spinney Hill, laid out in 1885-8; and then came the large Western Park, a consequence of the expansion across the river, in 1901.

So much for open-air recreation. Indoors, among formal entertainments, the drama had the primacy, but it was never distinguished. The new theatre of 1836 (it seems to have been called the Theatre Royal officially from 1851) was in the hands of a long series of lessees, none of whom made much profit from his enterprise.[2] A rival, the Amphitheatre, was erected in 1840 in Humberstone Gate. Large and flimsy, it held nearly 3,000 people. It failed as a theatre – it was offered for sale within a year of its opening[3] – and after serving a number of other uses it was demolished in 1848. This competition probably damaged the Theatre Royal, which was put on the market by its original owners in 1847. Within a dozen years of its opening it might well have passed out of theatrical use for good: for the Corporation seriously considered purchasing it to form a museum. The Proprietory School was, however, preferred for this purpose, and the theatre continued, in new hands. Some famous actors played there: Charles Kean (with very moderate acceptance) in the opening season, Helen Faucit, Barry Sullivan, Henry Irving. But throughout the Victorian age the arrangements were discontinuous and haphazard. There was nearly always a Christmas pantomime, the advertisements of

---

[1] Calculation from Storey, 121–4.
[2] Cf. R. Leacroft, 'The Theatre Royal, Leicester': 34 TLAS (1958) 39–52; Billson, *Leicester Memoirs*, 115–20.
[3] *Leicester Chronicle*, 8 May 1841.

each proclaiming its superiority, in mechanism and visual splendour, to all that had gone before.[1] For the rest, the Theatre did not always present the drama at all. It might accommodate a wild animal show, a masquerade, a moving 'Panorama' depicting the journey from St Louis to 'the Great Gold Fields and Cities of California'. At the opposite end of the scale, and most surprisingly, it presented one of the first English performances of *Carmen* in 1879, and that was received with delight.

The imperfect success of the Theatre Royal was due partly to faults of design. Its acoustics were severely criticised when it was new. It was thoroughly remodelled in 1873, and again in 1888: improved perhaps, but still not to the point where it could make itself continuously profitable. The man who planned the alterations of 1873, Eliot Galer, then agreed to lease a new and much larger theatre himself: the Opera House in Silver Street, opened in 1877. He may have considered the Theatre Royal (Plate 18a), which held about 1,300 people, uneconomically small. The new theatre was twice that size. 'Rather beyond the immediate requirements of Leicester' was the damping comment of a not unsympathetic townsman.[2] True enough: yet Galer retained his lease for many years, so presumably he made some kind of living from it, in part at the expense of the Theatre Royal. Clearly the town could not support two theatres – still less three, when the Palace appeared, for variety shows (lavishly decorated in the Moorish style) in 1900.[3] It could scarcely support one. As the circuit system developed early in the twentieth century, both the Theatre Royal and the Opera House found places on it, to accommodate touring companies for a week at a time. It must have been then that the melancholy theatrical proverb became current: that there were three disastrous weeks in the theatre – the week before Christmas, Holy Week, and a week in Leicester.

The theatre did not flourish in the town at any time, except perhaps early in the seventeenth century. Is that a consequence of its abiding Puritanism? The question is unanswerable. Though Nonconformist preachers in Leicester attacked the theatre, they did that elsewhere too. But if no exact evidence is available, we are still entitled to guess; and it is an obvious truth that a town like Victorian Leicester, dominated by Dissent and Evangelical Churchmanship, was not a place in which the theatre was likely to find intelligent and liberal patronage.

The good musical tradition that the town had established in the Georgian age languished under Victoria. There were subscription concerts from time to time, and we hear occasionally of the visits of prominent musicians, like Patti and Sims Reeves; but nothing emerges of the least interest or distinction. The usual standard

[1] Cf. J. Simmons, *Life in Victorian Leicester* (1971), 22.
[2] Read, 217.
[3] 35 TLAS (1960) 48.

is indicated, one fears, by a 'Grand Evening Concert' in 1838, at which Signor Puzzi performed a souvenir of *Lucia di Lammermoor* on the French horn, followed by a double fantasia on the horn and harp entitled 'Vous et Moi' and, as a triumphant ending, a 'Musical Effusion in honour of H.M. The Queen'.[1] From such tomfoolery it is a relief to turn to the lively music made in a public house: the Rainbow and Dove in Northampton Street, kept by Samuel Cleaver, where glees and traditional English songs were to be heard for many years, on a highly organised basis, the company joining in.[2] For musical performances requiring a large auditorium, only the Temperance Hall in Granby Street was available, until just before the First World War.

The mention of the Rainbow and Dove reminds us that the public houses were the chief sources of popular amusement throughout the Victorian age, and indeed until the arrival of television in the 1950s. The pubs and beer shops (or, as we now call them, off-licences) of Leicester were innumerable. One wonders if even the licensing justices could accurately count them all. A total of 141 are listed in a directory of 1815. Twenty years later the figure has risen to 223, besides 136 beer shops. In 1869 the total number of establishments that sold strong drink in the town was said to be 545.[3] By that time the range of attractions they could offer had become larger. The more prosperous places now included saloons – much disapproved of by moral reformers, who tried to counter such influences by setting up working men's clubs in separate premises.

The control of the sale of liquor greatly troubled the Victorian citizens; understandably, for drunkenness and common assault are leading elements in almost every police report. The temperance movement, in various guises, found influential supporters in Leicester; many of its leading citizens, indeed, associated themselves with it. One of its memorials was the Leicester Temperance Building Society, which was founded in 1875. Not all temperance men advocated total abstention. Joseph Dare, who clamoured for the licensing laws to be tightened and thoroughly rejoiced in the Act of 1872, nevertheless disapproved of prohibition and, when he established a working men's club, wisely permitted beer to be sold there.[4]

For all the energy of the reformers – whether doctrinaire fanatics or moderate, sensible men – the pubs flourished.[5] And when all has been said, they deserved to do

[1] *Leicester Journal,* 27 December 1838.
[2] Read, 217–8.
[3] Fowler, *Leicester Directory* (1815), 60–3; *Pigot & Co.'s Directory* (1835), 136–7; 24 RLDM 8.
[4] 10 *ibid.* 5; 21 *ibid.* 6–7.
[5] For their role as centres of the carrying trade see *Perspectives in English Urban History,* ed. A. M. Everitt (1973), 227–8.

so. Much crime was hatched in them, no doubt; there was rowdiness outside them, and brutality at home when they closed on Saturday nights. Yet they provided almost the only common meeting-place, off the streets, and their crude rough hospitality was often the only element of joy that working men knew in their ordinary lives. It is sad to think that, what with the city's modern redevelopment and the lavish expenditure of the brewers, only a few fragments of these Victorian pubs have survived today. For they played an intimate and vital part in this increasingly prosperous town.

9

There is one other activity of the Victorians that can properly be seen as an amusement, though it was very much a part of the serious daily routine of life: the business of shopping. It was not in any way a new business – we have seen a little of it in earlier times (cf.i.111). But it is only at this point, in the later nineteenth century, that we begin to have much information about it, enabling us to see what the shops were like, what goods they sold, what they charged, and what service they offered. For many women in the town they provided not only the source of their necessities, but the sole equivalent they ever knew of picture galleries and clubs. Let us look at the Victorian shops of Leicester, in part at least, through these women's eyes.

The whole of the markets' retail business now came to be concentrated on a single site, with the closing of the ancient open market in High Cross Street, latterly confined to the sale of fruit and vegetables, in 1884, and its transfer to the main Market Place. So, after about five centuries (and in the teeth of a fierce opposition from some of the residents in High Cross Street),[1] the Wednesday and Saturday market places were at length combined. On busy days the stalls filled the spaces in front of the Corn Exchange and on both sides of it. The sale of fish and meat was brought under cover, a Fish Market being constructed in 1877.

There had been shops around the Market Place for centuries past, with living-rooms above: unusually tall and narrow for Leicester, in testimony to the high value of land there. Many of them were rebuilt, though by no means all: if one looks today above the fascia line of the shops one can still count four or five pre-Victorian buildings. The commercial premises of some of them now extended up to the first floor and even higher, like the Royal Hotel and Adderly's, which became for a time the most highly esteemed of all the Leicester drapers, an embryo department store. That kind of large shop, unheard of previously, now began

[1] Storey, 133–4.

to be developed in Leicester. To its smaller neighbours it presented the same kind of threat as that of the supermarket to their successors in our own time. Adderly's has gone; but we can still get an idea of the kind of building that was thought appropriate for the purpose from what is now Fenwick's, on the corner of Belvoir Street and Market Street – in earlier days, Joseph Johnson's. The timbered balcony at the top, placed diagonally, gives the whole edifice an amusing touch of fantasy. It reflects the romance of commerce, as the later Victorians saw it.

The growth in the size of shops, and the adoption of plate-glass for the windows they used for displaying their goods, gradually changed their architecture. Lock-up shops, with living accommodation above them, began to be erected in terraces. A series of these remains today, little changed, at 110–20 Granby Street.[1] Not far away, in Belvoir Street, the corner building at the junction with Albion Street (now Young's, the chemist's) was chosen by a German student at the turn of the century as an example of good commercial architecture in England. Above the ground-floor level, it is exactly as it was when it was photographed for his book.[2]

And yet how hard it is to reconstruct for ourselves the appearance and design of the Victorian shops of Leicester! Some survived little altered until quite lately, but have now been despoiled: the Beehive in Cank Street, for instance, Morley's lamented draper's shop in Cheapside – Richard Morley's initials are still to be seen in its iron balcony. Nearly next door to Morley's stands Blackman's tobacco shop, which was established in 1869 and is practically untouched, with shutters, and windows protected by spick and span brass fenders; but things of that kind are now rare in the middle of the modern city. Away from the centre there are some that are well worth finding. Hind's, the large and busy chemist's in Queen's Road, Clarendon Park, has much of the furniture of the original pharmacy designed for it when it was opened in 1888. It all adds greatly to the interest and pleasure of doing business there today. There are few photographs of Victorian shops in use, crowded with goods, presided over by deferential managers and assistants, like those whom Arnold Bennett immortalised in *The Old Wives' Tale*.

The lives of the men and women who worked in these shops were often hard, and not very cheerful. Towards the end of the century some shopkeepers began to close for a half-day each week to give their employees a little rest. Richard Morley's son was a pioneer in this practice, announcing in the 'eighties that his shop closed at two o'clock on Thursdays;[3] but this did not become a general rule until it was made compulsory by legislation in 1912.

By the end of the century the leading shops and business houses in the town were

[1] An architect's elevation is reproduced in Simmons, *Life in Victorian Leicester*, Plate 9.
[2] H. Muthesius, *Die englische Baukunst der Gegenwart* (1900), 57, Plate 13. The building was not new when Muthesius published his book; it bears the date 1887.
[3] Advertisement in C. N. Wright, *Directory of Leicester* (1888), 627.

coming to equip themselves with the telephone. The National Telephone Company's Directory for 1891 shows a total of 158 subscribers, including most of the leading commercial names (though only two hotels and one doctor). The inconvenience of the dual system under which the private company and the Post Office operated side by side, with the Post Office controlling all trunk lines, disturbed the Chamber of Commerce, which consistently supported the acquisition of the whole system by the Government.[1]

Leicester certainly turned itself into a good shopping centre in the later Victorian age. It began with the great advantage of its large and well-administered markets. Their trade was now fostered by an extensive system of carriers' services. In the 'eighties, it has been calculated, two-thirds of the villages in Leicestershire enjoyed that convenience, with an average frequency of five services a week.[2] The development of its railway system helped to make Leicester one of the chief points of distribution in the trade of the country at large. The footwear industry is a conspicuous and special case; but there are others of a much more general kind. For example Currys Ltd, who are today a London firm known far and wide as distributors of electrical appliances, originated in Leicester, in premises on Belgrave Gate opened in 1884; Halfords started in Halford Street in 1901. As time went on, shopkeepers became more and more alive to the importance of drawing in custom from outside the town; and the clearance sale, with its promise of bargains, has a long history behind it. Here, for instance, is the Furniture Supply Co., advertising such a sale and promising to pay the railway fare of every customer who spent £2 or more in the shop.[3] What makes this especially interesting is that this firm's premises were in the newly-rebuilt High Street and cannot have been open much more than a year at the time. We are not far away from the common modern practice of opening a new cheap shop with a sale.

The devices that the shops adopted for advertising their wares changed markedly in the course of the Victorian age. They are an invaluable storehouse of information on the history of retail trade in the town.[4] One can listen to an endless variety of overtones in them, from straight calculation to the remotest blandishments of snobbery. Snobbery indeed entered largely into the whole business, not only in the

[1] 39th Report (1899), 15.
[2] Cf. Prof. Everitt's interesting analysis in *Perspectives in English Urban History*, 221, 226, 236–40.
[3] *Leicester Chronicle*, 20 February 1904.
[4] Invaluable, and quite incomprehensibly neglected. Retail trade (except in markets and fairs) is a subject totally ignored by the *Victoria County History*, in Leicester as elsewhere. Dissertations, theses, and books could all be profitably devoted to it, with the guidance of two admirable recent works: D. Alexander, *Retailing in England during the Industrial Revolution* (1970), and the comprehensive *History of Shopping* by Mrs Dorothy Davis – herself now a citizen of Leicester.

approach made to the customer but in the shopkeeper's very decision to advertise at all. It is only towards the close of the age that the leading firms consent to proclaim their wares in the newspapers. That is particularly true of such businesses as drapery; less true perhaps of wine merchants, though even there it is noticeable that the top firms like Hollingworth's remain reticent. Conversely, Herbert Marshall founded the expansion of his very successful business as a maker of pianos and other musical instruments largely on advertising, of relentless pertinacity. And his advertisements enable us to see the emergence of hire purchase in Leicester; one more sign of prosperity, and of a departure from the older notions of thrift.[1]

Those notions were still very much alive, however. The Leicester Trustee Savings Bank (founded in 1817) had weathered a bad period in the 'forties, when for some time withdrawals had exceeded deposits, to achieve a sound continuous security. In 1873 it was able to erect a Gothic building for itself on the corner of St Martin's and Grey Friars, then a new street. Four years later it began to open for business on every weekday.[2] There were two building societies in the town, each founded at a moment of affluence: the Permanent, dating from 1853, the Temperance from 1875.[3] In 1974 they were amalgamated to form a single Leicester Building Society.

10

The first impression Leicester gives a visitor is one of a rosy-red town set in a mass of greenery; owing to the absence of good building stone and the presence of excellent brick clay, the town is honestly and unaffectedly one of red brick; and recognising the beauties as well as the limitations of its material, its architects have developed a local school of art in brick, which is at least commendably free from the fussiness and flamboyancy too often associated with the use of this material.[4]

These are the words of Alfred Harvey, an antiquary with an eye for something besides the old. They were written in 1912, and then they were exactly right. But nothing of the kind would have occurred to any one who had looked at Leicester

[1] Simmons, *Life in Victorian Leicester,* 57–8.
[2] Cf. G. P. Cave and J. Martin, *Leicester Trustee Savings Bank,* 1817–1967 (n.d.).
[3] The original rules of the Permanent Society are in LRLP vol. 36, of the Temperance in vol. 38.
[4] *Little Guide to Leics. and Rutland* (1912), 107–8.

fifty years before. During that half-century – the time surveyed in this chapter – its physical appearance was decisively changed.

By the 1860s brick building was invading the Old Town in force. With every year that went by, more brick warehouses and factories were being erected there, more commercial premises rebuilt in brick, or at least refaced in it. A good deal of the ancient lath-and-plaster building survived – though even that was now very often patched or in-filled with brick; and some stucco fronts still helped to give variety of colour and texture to the streetscape.[1] By 1914 hardly any of this continued to be visible, and what little did remain was often vilely treated – like the old Grammar School in High Cross Street (vol. i, Plate 15a), which became the warehouse of a Kidderminster carpet manufacturer in the 'seventies[2] and remained in the occupation of his successors for almost 100 years.

Outside the Old Town, in the huge districts that were then being developed, red brick universally prevailed. With one exception. New churches were built predominantly of stone: the coarse local stone from Charnwood Forest, as in Gilbert Scott's St John the Divine, Ewan Christian's St Mark's, Ordish's St Leonard's; good limestone where it could be afforded, as in the spire of St Martin's. It was the combination of these two stones together that formerly gave Street's St Peter's, in the then prosperous Highfields, its special distinction (see Plate 3). The Nonconformists generally continued the appropriate and pleasing tradition of the red-brick meeting-house inherited from their founders in the seventeenth century, though they too had their extravagances, where the will and the money were present. Especially the Baptists, anxious perhaps to publish the power they had won in the community in succession to the austerer Unitarians: in the Gothic church on the corner of what is now University Road and London Road, in the strident polychrome brick of their chapel in Friar Lane. (That was built in 1866, to commemorate the bicentenary of the establishment of the denomination in the town. What *would* the first sober Baptists of Leicester have said if they could have seen it? It was a monstrosity, and it has now been destroyed in favour of the motor-car.)

The Anglicans also used red brick on occasion: Scott for instance at St Andrew's and St Saviour's; Bodley too, with great restraint, in one of his last works – the most refined religious building erected anywhere in Leicester since the Reformation, All Souls on the Aylestone Road. But compare the brickwork at St Andrew's and All Souls (they lie only ten minutes' walk apart). The difference between them – the pungent vermilion, redolent of the 'seventies, and Bodley's subtle, subdued pinkish-brown – is a good demonstration of the great range of colour and texture that the material can afford.

[1] See some of the pictures reproduced in 36 TLAS (1960) 45–8, especially Plates 3, 23, 24.
[2] Read, 273–4.

Not all the brick produced in and around Leicester was red. A particularly agreeable buff-grey, shot with yellow and pink, was used for facing the Asylum[1] in 1836–7. This brick may have been made near at hand: there were brickyards all along the hill, adjoining the Victoria Park and below it, until they were swept away by an enlargement of the Cemetery in 1874.[2] That possibility is strengthened by the appearance of similar brick in houses in the New Walk and Welford Road. When the Asylum building was extended towards the back in the 1840s a much harsher yellow brick was employed. Can it have come from Ibstock, by the Leicester and Swannington Railway?

For the rest it was red brick everywhere, which might be imported by rail from any part of England. The truly affectionate citizen of Leicester must recognise that and observe it closely, in all its varieties and gradations. The leading characteristic of its treatment was — most properly in this town – sobriety. And one of the impulses that lay behind its adoption was moral, a consideration particularly congenial to the age and place. To use brick, unmasked by the stucco favoured under the Regency, was to use 'honest material in an honest way; leaving truthfulness in this as in other things to assert its supremacy over shams and imitations'.[3] Such ethical and aesthetic arguments were supported – one might say clinched – by the repeal of the brick tax in 1850.

Among all the great towns of Britain Leicester thus became, with perhaps the exception of Stoke-on-Trent, the one in which red brick predominated most strongly.

But Harvey drew attention to two things: to that and to the trees. It was the combination of them both that gave the town its special charm. Where trees were absent, and the red brick left bare, there was no charm at all; and that alas was true of the majority of the small streets of terraced houses, most notably perhaps those built off the Belgrave Road in the 'seventies and 'eighties. Where trees were planted, and still more where they were established and allowed to remain, they provided the perfect foil for the red brick beside them. The great exemplar was the London Road in Stoneygate, where the big brick houses were embedded in trees, shading their gardens and screening them from the traffic that passed. Many of them were very large, and sensitively preserved. It was a distinction of Stoneygate, in contrast to the opulent late-Victorian quarters in many other towns, that its predominant trees were deciduous. The baneful conifer was miraculously rare, apart from a few noble cedars, carefully cherished survivals from an earlier age.

[1] Now the Fielding Johnson Building of the University.
[2] Storey, 54.
[3] 4 TLAS (1878) 132. Cf. 2 ibid. (1870) 289; also A. Clifton-Taylor, *The Pattern of English Building* (1972 ed.), 228, 369.

But if that stretch of the London Road was the chief spectacle of Leicester, the town had many smaller streets in which trees were planted: Howard Road, in Clarendon Park, for instance. How did this come about? Who was responsible? London Road may have set a tone. It is possible that one of the Mid-Victorian Surveyors – the humdrum Stephens or the remarkable Gordon – had an eye for these things and used his influence where it was effective. We cannot tell. But one other thing certainly played its part: the established tradition of horticulture in the town. Long before its vast expansion began, the Old Town was a place of orchards and trees. At the very worst time, in the 1840s, J. R. Martin (i.170) noted 'numerous gardens' everywhere, even in its centre. (By contrast, the want of such ancient amenities helped to make the Wharf Street development dismal.) Allotments, too, arrived early in Leicester. William Biggs, good man, presided over an Allotment Society that had 860 members by 1845, 'who rent and cultivate 100 acres by spade husbandry'. At the same time a beginning was made – though impeded by legal difficulties – with setting out allotments on part of Freemen's Common.[1] Many open spaces, in the interstices of building, continued or were developed as market gardens and orchards. Avenue Road, for example (still incompletely built up today), had many fruit trees. A solicitor's clerk, Samuel Greatorex, raised a new apple there, Annie Elizabeth, for which John Harrison, a noted Leicester seedsman, was awarded a first-class certificate from the Royal Horticultural Society in 1868.[2]

The combination that characterised later Victorian Leicester, of the red and the green, may therefore be said to have arisen from the very spirit of the place. The resulting beauty was of a homely sort. When the challenge to construct something large came, it was usually met with incomplete success. And that too is what might be expected, for another reason. The town had never appreciated the formal, the elegant, or the grand.

By the 1860s the citizens were beginning to realise that the place was a deplorable muddle. Cautiously, they set out to tidy it up. The first sign of this effort was the building of the Clock Tower, which was intended to provide a traffic improvement, ludicrously overdue.[3] The assembly rooms of 1750, at the mouth of the High Street, had been demolished in 1862, and the coal that had been weighed on the ground floor of the building ceased to be sold there; the sale of hay and straw was removed from the Haymarket three years later. Two important obstructions were thus taken away, and the traffic was free to converge from six streets upon a large empty space. Horses, carriages, pedestrians, on market days livestock, all tumbled in, and the chaos was indescribable. Clearly the first thing

[1] W. White, *History, Gazetteer, and Directory of Leicestershire* (1846), 67.
[2] A. Simmonds, *A Horticultural Who Was Who* (1948), 24–5.
[3] 41 TLAS (1965–6) 47–9.

needed was some focal point around which all this traffic could revolve. The Clock Tower provided that, as well as a much-needed refuge for pedestrians. The initiative in erecting it came from a group of private citizens headed by the Radical John Burton, former editor of the *Leicestershire Mercury*. They subscribed the greater part of the cost. A competition was held for the design and won by Joseph Goddard. The Tower was completed in June 1868, and adorned with statues of public benefactors on the four corners (Plate 16a). It effected a real improvement. The credit for that was due to Burton and his friends, not to the municipality.

By this time it had become plain that a new Town Hall was essential.[1] The old Corporation had sought for it twice; the Improvers had been defeated in their effort to provide one in 1845. The matter came up again in the 'sixties, but progress was impeded by furious argument concerning the site and the accommodation the building should afford. A decision was reached at last in 1871 to erect it in Friar Lane. An architectural competition was held, in which the Corporation burnt its fingers, as many public bodies did then;[2] and the plan was abandoned. Late in 1872 the Council adopted a different site for the building, on the old Horse Fair. There was a fresh competition, with T. H. Wyatt as the architectural assessor. It was won by a little-known young architect, born in Leicester but practising in London, F. J. Hames. The building now at last got under way, and it was formally opened on 7 August 1876. It cost altogether a trifle less than £53,000.[3]

The result was something extraordinary: a transcendent demonstration of the spirit of the age, and of the town at its best (Plate 1). Inevitably, it was built of red brick. But the brick was not local; it came from Suffolk. The stone used for the window dressings was from Ketton in Rutland; most of that inside from Caen.[4] The form of the building was even less local in character. It owed something to the revival of interest in the architecture of Queen Anne's time, begun by John Shaw and Nesfield; something also, in its clock tower, to Flanders. The eclecticism of the Victorians was often disastrous. Hames vindicated it here in triumph, to achieve subtle variety within an entirely coherent whole. It is one of the best public buildings of its age; and the Corporation deserves full credit for accepting a design well in advance of the fashion – perhaps, in a sense, outside it.

In one respect alone it was disappointing. Hames was asked to lay out the

---

[1] The inconveniences of the old one are summarised in 27 *Builder* (1869) 451, 531.
[2] Cf. for example 6 *Architect* (1871) 14–15, 37–8, 40, 82, 221; 29 *Builder* (1871) 541.
[3] On Hames's designs see 10 *Architect* (1873) 29–30, 37–8; 31 *Builder* (1873) 141, 431, 477–8; 24 *Building News* (1873) 476. Statement of accounts in Storey, 69.
[4] 37 *Builder* (1879) 1209.

ground in front of the new building; and presently Israel Hart gave the money to erect a fountain there, which again Hames designed, with success. But it remained no more than an open space, not quite big enough for the scale of the Town Hall, and lined with a congeries of buildings, disparate in height and shape. One sighs for John Johnson's Brunswick Square (i.139): a true square indeed, in the metropolitan manner of its time. In one thing, however, the new Square was satisfactory. It was all built of red brick. If the houses were an undistinguished miscellany, they were right in scale; and when new buildings were put up they were right too – most notably the Sun Alliance Assurance Building erected by Goddard's firm in 1891, an exhibition piece of Victorian craftsmanship at its best in brick, stone, and slate.[1]

With the new Town Hall at length available, all business was immediately transferred there from the old. Need it be said that Hames's building was soon found to be inadequate in size? A new one was in contemplation by 1897.[2] The ancient building stood empty, except for the old town library, which remained in its original quarters. It would have been natural to pull it down. That that did not happen may perhaps be due in part to the recent row over the demolition of Wyggeston's Hospital; in part to a vague feeling of discomfort among some of the Corporation at the idea of destroying what so patently embodied its history. Presently an odd use was found for the desolate building: to house the North Midland School of Cookery. The young women were taught to cook in the Great Hall, one class being divided from another by loosely-hung curtains. An old prison cell made a useful larder.[3] In these makeshift quarters, and others nearby, the School continued until 1921, when it was moved, under the title of the Leicester Domestic Science College, to premises constructed for it in Knighton Fields. The Guildhall then reverted to silence, broken only when a rare visitor stepped aside to look at it, or at the books in the library.

After the Town Hall, no major public building was erected for nearly thirty years. The next was the new Library, designed by a Leicester architect, Edward Burgess, to harmonise with Hames's building on the opposite side of Bishop Street.[4] It was followed in 1913 by an edifice of quite another kind.

One of the town's most obvious deficiencies was a large hall for public meetings. The Temperance Hall was the biggest available; but it was in private hands. The Corporation decided to remedy this want, by building a hall on the northern fringe of the Victoria Park. It was laid down that it was to be as cheap as possible; but at

[1] Leicester and Leics. Soc. of Architects, 1874 *Report* 4; 72 *Builder* (1897) 497.
[2] Stevenson spoke up for it, and so did Hames, the architect of the new Town Hall: 17 *Architect* (1877) 56–8.
[3] *Guide to Leicester and District*, ed. G. C. Nuttall (1907), 57.
[4] Libraries Committee, 33 *Report* 6, 34 *ibid*. 7.

once there was uproar. No such hall was needed, or could be built with satisfactory acoustic properties; the maintenance of the building would be a constant drain on the rates.[1] The Corporation went ahead. The work was entrusted to the firm of Stockdale Harrison.[2] It was completed in 1913 and named the De Montfort Hall. The result was remarkable. For a low price – in the end, some £21,000[3] – the town got a hall capable of holding about 3,000 people: very broad, yet offering the occupant of almost every seat an unobstructed view; enriched with an impressive organ, the gift of Alfred Corah; and, as it turned out, acoustically superb for music. Quite unintentionally, Leicester found itself with what was beyond doubt the finest large concert hall in the Midlands; one of the finest, of its size, anywhere in England. Its one serious deficiency was not the architects' fault. Under pressure of economy, the artists' accommodation behind the stage was cut down, below a tolerable minimum. That blot has never been removed. In every other respect Leicester got a splendid new asset; and the Corporation took pains with the setting of the hall in flower gardens. With that addition adjoining it, the Victoria Park became as satisfactory as either of the newly-made parks to the north and west of the town.

The most impressive new commercial buildings erected in the Victorian age were the banks. By the middle of the nineteenth century, after many failures and amalgamations, there were three local banks left in the town. Two of these were joint-stock banks, Pares's and the Leicestershire Banking Company; the third a private house, Paget's. In addition, there was a branch of the National Provincial Bank, opened in 1836; and the Bank of England had a branch in Leicester from 1844 to 1872.[4] Though all these banks, of such widely different kinds, prospered (there were no further failures among them), their operations were on a quite small scale. They did not need large offices. The first such offices in Leicester were erected not by one of the local firms but by the National Provincial Bank, which put up a handsome Italianate building in 1869 (Plate 7a) on the site of the Three Crowns, just then demolished, at the junction of Horsefair Street and Granby Street. Thereupon the Leicestershire Banking Company determined to go one better. A few doors away along Granby Street it erected a Venetian Gothic building in 1871, clearly intended to make its rival look old-fashioned. Designed by Joseph Goddard, both in materials and in style it had the courage of entire

---

[1] 101 *Builder* (1911) 635.

[2] For the partnership of Stockdale and Shirley Harrison cf. L. L. Smith and R. J. B. Keene, *1872–1972: the First Hundred Years of the Leicestershire and Rutland Society of Architects* (1972), 10.

[3] The final cost exceeded the estimate by £3,800: *Council Minutes*, 1913–14, 303–6.

[4] For the history of banking in Leicester cf. VCHL iii. 50–6 and Billson, *Leicester Memoirs*, 1–34.

conviction. We can appreciate that today, since the Midland Bank, which now owns it, has recently cleaned it with care, to reveal the vermilion brickwork as it was when it was new. On the Granby Street front Goddard introduced pretty panels of terracotta.[1] This seems to be its first appearance in the middle of the town.

The banks now began to become, what they are so notably today, the sensitive weathercocks of architectural vogue. In Leicester, in these two instances, they did well. They did even better in the next generation, when Perkins Pick built new headquarters for Pares's Bank in St Martin's in 1901. The building has a noble amplitude, a dignity kept from becoming pompous by the small touches of *art nouveau* in the metalwork and expressed to perfection in its white Portland stone. The banking hall inside is quite as fine; one hopes it will never be altered. In the very next year after the building was completed, at a cost of nearly £40,000, Pares's Bank passed into the hands of Parr's in London; and so it too – like the National Provincial – has become part of the National Westminster Bank today.[2]

Among other commercial buildings one thinks first, in a town like this, of factories, mills, and warehouses. It was in the 'sixties and 'seventies – late and with some reluctance – that the making of hosiery came to be undertaken in factories. In accordance with the whole history of the trade, they were mostly small and unimpressive. With one conspicuous exception.

Having conquered many handicaps, Nathaniel Corah had established a hosier's business in 1815. It was closely connected with Birmingham, where he opened a warehouse in Moor Street in 1828. After his death four years later his sons built larger premises in Granby Street, equipped with a steam engine. Other small factories were added to it until in 1865 the firm determined to concentrate all its activities in Leicester into a single set of buildings. It acquired four acres of land just east of St Margaret's church and erected a carefully-planned factory (including a recreation ground for the workers), which was brought into use in 1866. With an astonishing flourish of extravagance, the building was 'surmounted by a colossal figure of Commerce' in Box stone.[3] Within twenty years the firm was employing 1,000 people.

The footwear manufacture produced no comparable monument, though one solidly handsome building was put up in 1870 by Stead & Simpson's at the south end of Belgrave Gate.[4] Freeman Hardy & Willis's premises, capacious but archi-

[1] Goddard had already used it for decorative details in a house in the South Fields: 6 *Architect* (1871) 307.
[2] It is described in 81 *Builder* (1901) 252.
[3] J. M. Wilson, *Imperial Gazetteer of England and Wales* [?1869], ii. 3. Cf. K. Jopp, *Corah of Leicester* [1965].
[4] Cf. R. Moore in LM 9 October 1970.

tecturally undistinguished, were in Rutland Street. Further along that same street was the elastic-web factory of Faire Bros, completed in 1898. The architect there was Burgess, and he faced the entire building in soapy yellow terracotta. The *Builder* considered this – as perhaps we do not – 'a really delightful example of the appropriate and pleasing use' of that material.[1] Terracotta was indeed fashionable in the 'nineties. It was to be seen again adorning the façade of the new Midland Railway station in 1892; and (applied with less variety) on the Wyvern Hotel, the work of Arthur Wakerley, an architect who left his chief mark away from the centre of Leicester (cf. p. 121).

The Wyvern was a large temperance establishment, immediately adjoining the station to the north. Leicester was true to itself in the greeting it offered to visitors. It was the only town of its size, north of the Thames, that lacked a station hotel in the hands of a railway company or its lessees.[2] The stranger, arriving in Leicester by the Midland Railway in 1900, saw nothing but one temperance hotel; and if he walked down Granby Street the first thing he came upon was another Thomas Cook's. With perseverance, however, he could reach the Grand, an imperial pile just completed to the designs of Cecil Ogden in 1898.

The town had no other major hotel. From the old coaching days the Bell survived, with a varying reputation. Matthew Arnold had found it in the 'sixties 'kept good by the hunting men';[3] later travellers were less pleased with it. But there was a profusion of 'coffee-houses' – another product of the temperance movement. Burgess specialised in designing them.[4] Though they have all been turned over to other uses long since, some of them are still extant as buildings: the East Gates, for example, on the corner of Churchgate (Plate 10b); the Victoria with its tall conical roof, black and gloomy now, in Granby Street.

Something has already been said of the private houses that were being built at this time. How can one possibly characterise them all, the 35,000 that went up between 1860 and 1914? They too followed fashions. Except for the small minority that were designed for the well-to-do, most of them were constructed in terraces: though one terrace might go up gradually over the years, a pair or two of houses at a time. Dated as they commonly were in the 'seventies and 'eighties, they often reflected in their names the thinking of those who built them: Cyprus Villa (recalling Disraeli's triumph in 1878); Eminence Cottages (surely built by a Roman Catholic: they belong to the year of Newman's elevation); Dasey Cottage

[1] 72 *Builder* (1897) 500.
[2] The Great Central Company took powers to erect one when its new line was being built through the town in the 'nineties (LPA 59 Vict. cap 207, sect. 30); but it never exercised them, as it did at Nottingham.
[3] *Letters*, ed. G. W. E. Russell (1895), i. 356.
[4] Cf. Muthesius, 116–17 and plates 66–7; 47 TLAS (1971–2) 55–61.

(the builder in 1891 was evidently illiterate: he meant Daisy); Thrums on the Hinckley Road (its erection followed Barrie's book by some six years).[1] One house in Knighton Drive bears nothing but the enigmatic inscription 'In Memoriam'.

In houses where an architect was employed, Tudor and Jacobean influence was strong. A few of those in Stoneygate caught the attention of the technical press: Elmsleigh in London Road for instance, in 1874, Knighton Spinneys, which Joseph Goddard built for himself in Ratcliffe Road.[2] A drawing of Isaac Barradale's showing his cottages on the St Barnabas estate was shown at the Royal Academy in 1888.[3] But the truest originality went unnoticed. In 1892 Ernest Gimson built himself a house in Ratcliffe Road, naming it Inglewood. He followed it five years later by the White House, for his brother Arthur, in North Avenue. Though Gimson came of a family deeply rooted in Leicestershire, he worked very little in Leicester itself. He was still a young man at this time. In the end he found his *métier* not in architecture but in the design and making of furniture. The influence of William Morris, whom he met in 1884, may well have been more fruitful through him than through any one else: rejecting mechanical production entirely, he 'brought to furniture-making the individual genius it had lacked since the death of Sheraton'.[4] He continues to be commemorated in Leicester:[5] in important pieces of his work in the City Museums (Plate 14b), and in these two houses. Inglewood is especially memorable. Quiet, unpretending, beautifully made, it has nothing whatever to do with 'style'. It is timeless.

To turn from a Gimson house to those designed by the successful practitioners of the age is to move into another world. (Look at Knighton Lodge, which adjoins Inglewood in Elms Road.) But though they were lesser men, their work is not to be despised: especially when it can still be seen in the spacious garden setting that Leicester people felt at home in. Some of the best remaining examples are the houses built by the firm of Stockdale Harrison in the opening years of the twentieth century, just beyond the limits of the borough, in Oadby. The University has now acquired most of them and, as far as it can afford to do so, it maintains their

[1] For the curious, these houses are 11 Central Avenue, 5–11 Avenue Road Extension, 280 Clarendon Park Road, and 181 Hinckley Road respectively. Before we poke fun at the Victorians for the names they gave their houses, let us recognise that they are quite free from the archness and whimsy that have become common in our own century: cf. Folkdom (2 Beechcroft Road) or Ma Wee Hoose (259 Knighton Church Road).
[2] 32 *Builder* (1874) 130, 132.
[3] 55 *ibid.* (1888) 414.
[4] J. Gloag, *English Furniture* (2nd edn, 1946), 132. Sir Nikolaus Pevsner describes him as 'the greatest of the English artist-craftsmen': *Pioneers of Modern Design* (Pelican edn), 152.
[5] Though not always elsewhere as he ought to be: he belongs to the small company of really distinguished men who are not included in the *Dictionary of National Biography*.

gardens (Plate 22a). None of them, even the largest, is in any respect ostentatious. Indeed the only really purse-proud house in the whole immediate neighbourhood of Leicester was Thurnby Court, erected in 1872 by J. A. Jackson, on the proceeds not of any local industry but of blockade-running in the American Civil War. It is said to have cost £250,000. Jackson himself was ruined by it, and most of it was demolished during the First World War.[1] That giant was a foreigner here.

All in all, Leicester made a pleasing impression at the turn of the century. Given new impetus and direction by the success of the Town Hall, its brick building tradition chimed exactly with the spirit of Norman Shaw and Ernest George. A knowledgeable German visitor wrote of it in 1900 as a place in which 'there is more good new architecture than one generally meets with in English towns of its size'.[2]

Leicester architects did not make great fortunes in these years. The richest of them seems to have been Wakerley, who left a gross estate of £128,000 when he died in 1931: but he also engaged in property development on a large scale (see p. 121). They organised themselves into a Society in 1872 as their legal brethren had done in 1860, and the doctors very much earlier.[3] The Society of Architects strove to defend its members' interests as it saw them, protesting frequently against the rules laid down in competitions and trying to secure that local competitors only were admitted.[4] On the last point they were pretty successful. Apart from the Anglican churches, a special case, and the Town Hall (in which matter there was admittedly a grave infraction of the principle), only two major buildings were erected in the town in all these years to the design of outside architects: the London Road station, where the Midland Railway Company could cause no reasonable offence by employing its own architect, Charles Trubshaw, and Wyggeston's Hospital, whose buildings on the Fosse Road were due to T. C. Sorby. In this professional sphere there was, for the present, something very much like a closed shop.

II

So the big town got built, seemly in some respects, drab and hideous in others. It underwent a new series of upheavals, all coming close together, about the turn of

[1] VCHL v. 322.
[2] Muthesius, 116.
[3] The Leicester Medical Book Society, out of which the Medical Society grew, was founded in 1800 and is one of the oldest in England.
[4] Smith and Keene, *1872–1972*, 10–11, 12.

the century. The Great Central Railway strode across the western edge of the Old Town in 1899, on a blue-brick viaduct three-quarters of a mile long. It shouldered aside all the obstacles in its path, but in two important respects its development was controlled, in new ways. The plans, in the form they originally bore in 1890, provided for it to take the high ground east of the river, and therefore to smash straight through the Jewry Wall and the Castle. There was a loud and immediate outcry, in London as well as on the spot;[1] and, owing chiefly to the pertinacious protests of the Leicestershire Archaeological Society, the Company had to re-route the whole line, avoiding this vandalism by carrying it over the river and along its western bank. It was even forced to provide access for visitors to the Blackfriars Roman pavement, directly under its station platform.[2] Here was the first big battle in Leicester that the preservationists won. Indeed it had a national importance: for no other town had yet succeeded in forcing a railway company to change its course so substantially, in order to preserve ancient monuments.[3] But the passage of the railway not only threatened antiquities. Whatever route it took, it was bound to demolish houses and displace their occupants. They were not left to fend for themselves. The Company was obliged to re-accommodate them at its own expense, and it did so by building 300 houses on the Bow Bridge estate and at Newfoundpool.[4] This again was something relatively new: the protection of private citizens' interests when they were threatened by a commercial company. Since the houses destroyed were in one of the poorest quarters of the town, the railway made a useful, if involuntary, contribution to Improvement. At the same time a new street was cut to serve the station, called Great Central Street.

This railway, built at prodigious cost, did little to benefit the town. It is true that it broke the monopoly the Midland Company had long enjoyed in the services to London and Yorkshire. But there is scanty evidence that these existing services were found unsatisfactory. The Chamber of Commerce, for example, had voiced few complaints for many years.[5] Leicester was not, like some other towns, prominent in the attack on the railways during the controversy about rates in the 'eighties and 'nineties. The new company built an imposing goods warehouse south of its station. It probably offered a superior service for goods – as it certainly did, after 1900, for passengers – to Southampton and to South Wales. But there is

[1] 59 *Builder* (1890) 324.
[2] LPA 56 Vict. cap. 1, sect. 29 (17).
[3] See *The Victorian City*, ed. H. J. Dyos and M. Wolff (1973), i. 304, and references given there.
[4] G. Dow, *Great Central*, ii (1962), 318; L. T. C. Rolt, *The Making of a Railway* (1971), 24, 54–6, 83, 90, 118–20, 141, 148.
[5] It asked for an improvement in the service to Leeds in 1869 and got it (1869 *Report* 7); and it supported the Great Northern Company's endeavours to reach Leicester (1872 *Report* 8–9; 1873 *Report* 7; 1874 *Report* 5–6).

nothing whatever to show that it increased the town's prosperity. It was a splendid railway to look at, and agreeable to travel by; but in economic terms it was a total failure.

Another change in transport, which did a great deal for the town, was getting under way at the same time. The horse trams of the 'seventies, and the horse buses, had rendered a useful service, which we are apt to underestimate: in 1903 those trams carried 11 million passengers.[1] But in the closing years of the nineteenth century electric trams established their superiority in one town after another: Coventry had them from 1895, for example, Sheffield from 1899. It was not merely a matter of improved communication. Since most large municipalities now owned electricity undertakings, it was an economic advantage to them that they should have tramways using power they supplied themselves. Leicester had moved early in that matter, and then stopped dead in its tracks. As far back as 1879 it had been authorised to apply part of the capital of the gas undertaking, which it had acquired two years earlier, to electric lighting; but fifteen years went by before any of the town's streets were lit in that way.[2] When at last electricity works were built, on the premises of the Gas Department at Aylestone, they could be described in a London paper as 'among the finest in Britain'.[3] At last in 1901 the Corporation felt able to exercise its powers to buy out the private Tramways Company, with the intention of electrifying the system. Again it moved slowly. There was much argument going on about rival techniques and their technical and economic merits, and widespread dislike of the transmission of power by unsightly overhead wires. In the end, however, that was the system the Corporation decided to adopt; and it profited by waiting to learn from other people's experience. When the change came, it was put through rapidly: with one minor exception the whole system went over to electric operation between May and November 1904. The technical press applauded: this was regarded as 'one of the best and most modern systems in the country'.[4] The change brought immediate advantage to the rate-payers. The old private company had done well, seldom paying a dividend of less than 5 per cent. The Corporation did better. In 1913, 37 million passenger journeys were made on the system, or 163 per head of the town's population, and the net profit was £20,000.[5] Such suburban railway traffic as there had been markedly diminished: the number of passengers booked at Humberstone Road station was halved between 1902 and 1910.[6] The electric trams carried everything

---

[1] M. S. W. Pearson, *Leicester's Trams in Retrospect* (n.d.), 66.
[2] Storey, 102–4.
[3] 68 *Builder* (1895) 405.
[4] Pearson, 13; 17 *Tramway and Railway World* (1905) 550.
[5] *Council Minutes*, 1913–14, 110.
[6] British Transport Historical Records MID 4/4 fol. 262v.; 4/5, fol. 286v.

before them. They did most to persuade people in Leicester to ride, instead of walking, to work, to the football match or the races, to shop in the middle of the town on Saturday afternoons.

By that time another change was under way, though the full significance of it had not yet appeared. Before the electric trams had started to run in Leicester, motor bicycles and cars had become a not uncommon sight. By 1 January 1904 eighty of these had been licensed by the County Borough of Leicester. Three months later the figure had more than doubled; there were then 104 motor-bicycles and 61 'other cars' belonging to the town.[1] Apart from electric trams and steam wagons, however, the public-service vehicles continued to be horse-drawn in 1914.

These developments, together with the relentless pressure of the growing population, called for some changes in the street system. Anticipating the electrification of the tramways, the Corporation determined to widen the High Street. This involved the removal of the last fragment of Lord's Place (i.99), an octagonal tower that still rose aristocratically, high above the roofs of its grubby commercial neighbours (Plate 11a). The new street that appeared in 1902–4 was a dreary place, enlivened only by Wakerley's Singer building at the western end, a jolly piece of commercial vulgarity.

At the same time another change occurred, which broke with the historic past. Two fairs were still held in the town, on terms granted in 1473, in May and October; pleasure fairs only now, without their old commercial significance, but noted events nevertheless and greatly enjoyed. They were accommodated on a strip called 'No Man's Land' on the south side of Humberstone Gate, with the stalls overflowing as far as the Market Place.[2] Such doings were incompatible with electric trams. The trams won, and the last fair was held in October 1902. The building line was then set back, and the town acquired the first street at its centre that could truly claim to be called wide.

Here then were many signs of an abundant prosperity: an opulent new railway, electric lighting and transport, new broader streets, a handsome Public Library and a Grand Hotel, a first-class concert hall; and coinciding with these, the end at last of the town's peculiar infant mortality. Since 1861 Leicester had moved, in population, from the twentieth place among the towns of the English provinces to the twelfth – the position it holds today. Yet here, as in the country at large, this was also a time of frustration and disturbance.

The Education Act of 1902 was fiercely resisted by Nonconformists, who contended that it was a device for saving the schools of the Church of England out of the rates. They brushed aside the great and genuine progress that the Act

[1] PP 1904 lxxix. 154–5.
[2] Billson, 114–15.

represented, in establishing a national system of secondary education and in improving the administration of the Act of 1870. (One wonders how much they really cared about those things. They were obsessed by their own grievances.) In Leicester, where Nonconformity was strong, protest against the Act was as fierce as we should expect. Like the anti-vaccinators, the Nonconformists welcomed the 'martyrdom' of being taken to court – this time for refusing to pay the education rate. At their head stood the Mayor, A. E. Sawday, who was fined by his fellow-magistrates in 1904.[1] This hubbub had only just begun to die down when it was succeeded by another protest, of a different kind.

The standard of living that prevailed in the town had unquestionably risen during the previous half-century, and it was continuing to rise. The 'lean stockinger' had ceased to be a figure in the streets. If employment was not continuously full, it was more readily available here, for women and men alike, than in most other comparable English towns. There was, however, much unrest in the footwear industry. That business was now concentrated almost entirely into factories. The workers were organised in a strong trade union, the National Union of Boot and Shoe Operatives, with its headquarters in Leicester; the employers had banded together too; and in 1892 a National Conference had been established, with Sir Thomas Wright as its neutral chairman, to arbitrate on conflicting claims in the industry. It failed to prevent a head-on collision in March 1895, with a lock-out lasting three weeks. Three out of four of the factories in the Leicester district were closed, and at one time as many as 22,000 workers were said to be unemployed.[2] The settlement, however – achieved in part through the mediation of Bishop Creighton of Peterborough and the Rev. James Mason (see p. 34) – proved lasting; and by 1900 the industry offered, in normal conditions, steady regular employment.

Such improvements naturally created their own expectations; and when the town felt, momentarily, a sharp recession in 1904–5, the disappointment and bitterness there were correspondingly strong. In June 1905 over 400 of the men unemployed in Leicester marched to London. The movement was organised by local Labour leaders, chiefly by Amos Sherriff and Jabez Chaplin, and the marchers were accompanied by the Vicar of St Mark's, the Rev. F. L. Donaldson, a latter-day Christian Socialist (Plate 13).[3] The demonstration may have contributed towards the passage of the Unemployed Workmen Bill that was then before Parliament: the Conservative measure that first authorised the setting-up of Labour Exchanges and paved the way for the work of Beveridge and the Liberals' insurance legislation of 1911.

[1] *Leicester Chronicle*, 30 January 1904.
[2] VCHL iv.321–4.
[3] *The Times*, 5, 10, 12, 19 June 1905.

In the general election of 1900 one of the two Members returned by Leicester was a Conservative. That strange event was due, as in 1860, to a split among the Liberals. At the next election in 1906 it could hardly be expected, whether in terms of local or of national feeling, that a Conservative would be successful again. He was turned out, in favour not of a Liberal however, but of a Labour candidate, Ramsay MacDonald. The old divisions within the Left had reappeared in a new form. The breach that opened grew steadily wider, and within twenty years Liberalism was a defeated force.

During the crisis of Parliamentary government in 1909–12, Leicester remained relatively quiet. There was of course much tub-thumping in the two elections of 1910, in which Nonconformist ministers were to the fore.[1] Militant suffragettes yelled and stamped. (Their bravest feat came later, in 1914, when they burnt down part of Blaby station.) But there were no serious disorders, political or industrial. Why, one wonders, should tempers apparently have cooled since 1905?

The answer must be suggested in economic terms. The recession had not continued long in Leicester. The progress of the engineering industry, so marked in the closing years of the nineteenth century, continued and was accelerated in the twentieth. The established firms developed and new ones arrived. Mr Gillette opened his first British factory at Leicester in 1905. Two years earlier the first typewriter made in the town had been put on the market. It was designed by a Spanish American, Hidalgo Moya, who had come over from the United States and had secured financial backing from a Leicester business man, J. G. Chattaway. The manufacture grew slowly, and Chattaway found it desirable to seek assistance. He was joined by J. W. Goddard and W. A. Evans, and together they established the Imperial Typewriter Co. Ltd in 1908. Its works were at first in Wharf Street, until in 1911 it erected new premises in North Evington (Wakerley's suburb).[2] The firm manufactured for a restricted but profitable market, specialising in machines whose keyboards could easily be removed and replaced by others with characters of a different language. By 1914, 95 per cent of the typewriters made in Leicester were exported.

These new branches of light engineering did not come to be sited in Leicester by any accident. Imperial Typewriters owed much to the Goddards, a family well established in a number of businesses in the town. And one of the common needs that bound all these manufacturers together was that they were able to make use, to an extent unusual in other branches of engineering, of the labour of women, so readily available in Leicester.

The diversification of industry had indeed done much to transform the town. But the transformation was not due to the new diversity alone. It arose from the

[1] VCHL iv. 240.
[2] Cf. *Making Imperial Typewriters* (n.d.).

very character of the industries themselves. A shrewd observer summarised much of that in two brief sentences when he remarked in 1898: 'Leicester makes no luxuries. That is one reason why it grows and thrives'.[1] One may doubt if, in the years 1860–1914, any large town in England grew and throve more.

12

Perhaps it may be allowable to take leave of Victorian Leicester in a series of those 'instantaneous photographs' that were among the most admired technical achievements of the age. Let us choose a few at random: of the detestable Earl of Cardigan, driving over from Deene, tearing like the maniac he was down the London Road hill to catch the night mail train from Campbell Street station, never with a minute to spare;[2] of James Glaisher, one of the founders of scientific meteorology, preparing to make a balloon ascent from Victoria Park but prevented by unsuitable weather, fleeing from the infuriated crowd determined to lynch him, to take refuge in the house of the Town Clerk, Samuel Stone;[3] of Thomas Hodges, elastic-web manufacturer, who had been so unfortunate as to lose his watch in a London brothel and so unwise as to institute a prosecution, arriving on the hustings in the Market Place as Mayor to announce the result of the election of 1868 and being greeted by the crowd swinging watches by their chains, calling out 'What's o'clock, Tommy, what's o'clock?';[4] of Mr Bills the confectioner and his gooseberry tarts that 'needed practice to negotiate successfully the streams of syrup that succeeded the first bite';[5] of William Morris coming to lecture to the Secular Society, staying with Sidney Gimson and arguing stoutly that he was not a poet or a dreamer, but a man of business – making for himself a disciple of the young Ernest Gimson, a son of the house, who put his doctrines into practice in ways that Morris himself never imagined.[6] These years have for us a continuing vitality that is all their own. They were the most successful years in the long history of Leicester.

[1] W. J. Gordon, *Midland Sketches* (1898), 129.
[2] J. Wake, *The Brudenells of Deene* (1953), 439–40.
[3] Ellis, *Records*, 197.
[4] Private information.
[5] Ellis, *Records*, 172.
[6] M. Morris, *William Morris* (1936), ii. 221.

II
Two World Wars

I

In Leicester, as in most other English towns, the first impression made by the declaration of war in 1914 was slight. The troubles in Ireland had seemed far more serious than those in the Balkans; nearer home, a threatened addition of a shilling to the rates was more immediately alarming. Putting such worries behind them, the townspeople had streamed out, according to what was now a well-established custom, to the seaside on 1 August, the Saturday before Bank Holiday, the 3rd. War was declared on Tuesday the 4th. There was a momentary pause. The Bank Holiday was extended to three days; and during those days many of the holiday-makers drifted back in bewilderment, without much idea of what had happened, and with no idea at all of what lay before them.

For the moment there was nothing for it but to obey the Government. Recruiting campaigns began at once. A thousand men were soon drilling on the Western Park. The old County Asylum building (disused since the removal of the patients to a new one at Narborough in 1907) was hastily swept out and cleaned, for conversion into a military hospital. Horses were requisitioned. Over 100 of the new motor vehicles were offered for national service.[1]

The town soon became involved in a bitter political argument, in personal terms special to itself. The Parliamentary Labour party was divided in its attitude towards the war. Ramsay MacDonald resigned its leadership before the first week was out. The line he took was confusing and appeared inconsistent. He was convinced that Britain should never have been dragged into the war, and he blamed Grey for the crime: 'he worked deliberately to involve us in war, using Belgium as

[1] F. P. Armitage, *Leicester, 1914–18* (1933), 13. Much of this section is based on Mr Armitage's book.

his chief excuse'.[1] Still, 'once war was declared and our brothers went out obedient to the call of duty, they had got to be supported'. How much clearer were the arguments of the out-and-out pacifists on one side, or on the other of J. H. Thomas, remonstrating with the railwaymen when they were considering a strike: 'This nation could have taken no other course than it did take as consistent with honour and safety. A strike at this stage would not be a strike against the companies, it would be a strike against the nation'.[2]

All the words just quoted were spoken in Leicester, which, because MacDonald represented it in Parliament, became a focal point in the debate that divided the Left throughout the war. To many people the place was thus rendered notorious. When a lad from Leicester was sent to serve far overseas, he said he got on well enough until his fellow-soldiers found out which was his home town. Thereupon they nicknamed him 'Ramsay' and treated him with contempt.[3] MacDonald's views were his own, warped and naïve at some points but sincerely held and declared with courage. He was repeatedly fortified by expressions of confidence from Leicester. A large majority of his constituents came to disapprove of him, however, and said so as soon as they got the chance. And yet the town as a whole showed itself a good deal less than enthusiastic in the prosecution of the war.

Recruiting in it was notably unsuccessful. At the outset in 1914 there was a rush to join up, as there was everywhere else, but it had died down by the end of September. In 1915 the backwardness of Leicester began to become a public scandal. When the Recruiting Committee itself met, many of its members failed to attend. In March things improved under the pressure of a special effort, as well as the stigma of a resolution adopted by the Town Council deploring 'the scanty response of Leicester men to the recruiting appeals'. The mover of the resolution pointed out that at Nottingham and Newcastle 18·5 per cent of the population had joined up, 6·7 per cent at Manchester and Sheffield, and at Leicester – 2·6. Even so, recruitment slackened off again. The explanation generally given was that those who had not volunteered were 'waiting to be fetched'. But the country was not yet ready for conscription; a great new effort was launched by the Government in the autumn to avoid it, with the appointment of Lord Derby as Director of Recruiting. A new appeal was made in October, and this time it succeeded. It was effectively managed and got off to a good start at a big meeting in the De Montfort Hall. The enthusiasm shown there was maintained. It was raised when news

---

[1] This scandalous travesty of fact was singled out for attack by Dr J. D. Freeman, Minister of the Belvoir Street chapel, in a series of ferocious letters published in the *Leicester Daily Post* on 29 July and 9–20 August 1915. MacDonald, on 9 August, sought to show that the meaning of this statement had been distorted. His defence on the point is unconvincing.
[2] Armitage, 14, 71, 75.
[3] *Ibid.*, 279.

arrived of the heroic part played by the 4th and 5th Leicesters in the taking of the Hohenzollern Redoubt on 13 October. Every one of the officers in the 4th Battalion was killed or wounded, with 453 other ranks. These casualties had plainly to be repaired. Many of them were local men. The emotional appeal now became strong, and it proved irresistible.[1]

The formal, and in many ways the actual, leadership of the town for nearly the whole of the war was exercised by Alderman Jonathan North. He took office as Mayor in November 1914 and was re-elected for three subsequent years – something that had last happened in the fourteenth century. He had not served in the office before, but as Chairman of Freeman Hardy & Willis (the largest firm of distributors in the British footwear trade) and of the Education Committee since 1905 he had had great and varied experience. Conscientious, hard-working, dignified, rather unimaginative, he carried a great burden throughout these years. He did his duty well.

The town did not have any exceptional hardships to suffer. No Zeppelin dropped bombs there – though they fell in Loughborough, killing ten people, in January 1916. In some directions its economy boomed. The Mayor's firm could pay a dividend of $17\frac{1}{2}$ per cent in 1916, give a wage bonus of 5 per cent to its workers, and set aside £3,000 for charity.[2] Inflation began, and presently its pace accelerated; but wages seemed to rise in proportion. From time to time there were what were described as 'orgies of spending' – early in 1916, at Christmas 1917, for example.[3] Attempts to revive the dying virtue of thrift and to direct it into war savings, to the advantage of the country as a whole, met a cool response: the town did not find all its allotted share of the Victory Loan of 1917 – though it did better when other special appeals were made a year later.[4]

The rationing of food in this war was an oddly haphazard business. Nationally, it was introduced in great haste early in 1918, chiefly as a device for allaying discontent. But there were already many local arrangements, and Leicester had some that were of interest. On the orders of a well-managed Food Control Committee, the rationing of butter and margarine was introduced (apparently for the first time in an English town) in 1917; sugar was rationed from 1 January 1918, and meat (here again Leicester seems to have been a pioneer) in the following month. A local plan for coal rationing, to take account also of the consumption of gas and electricity, was devised in the last summer of the war. The prices of food were controlled, not very effectively: it paid the farmers to send milk to London, for

[1] *Ibid.*, 24–30, 86–93. Cf. J. Milne, *Footprints of the 1/4th Leicestershire Regiment* (1935), 54–6; J. D. Hills, *The Fifth Leicestershire* (1919), 83.
[2] Armitage, 126.
[3] *Ibid.*, 147, 213.
[4] *Ibid.*, 203–5, 266–70.

example, because the dairymen there were willing to give them 2d. a gallon above the controlled price. Some shopkeepers were fined in Leicester for charging more than was allowed; it is plain that there was continual irregularity.[1] All this was pointed out, naturally enough, by women in food queues and by men on soap boxes. But though there was much grumbling and some unrest, especially in 1918, there were no strikes, and no disturbances worth the name. The prevailing mood came to be one of dejection, dominated by the appalling casualty lists and, as the war moved into its fifth year and hope after hope had proved delusive, very little relieved by real confidence in victory.

With the success of the Allies at Amiens in August 1918, everything began to change. In three months the war was over. In Leicester its termination was announced at two o'clock on 11 November by the Mayor, Walter Lovell, who had just succeeded North, and by North himself, who spoke of the need to make sacrifices in gratitude to the men who had fought.

The relief at the ending of the war was marred by the fierce epidemic of influenza that accompanied the closing months of the struggle. It hit Leicester first in June and July 1918; then, much harder, in the autumn, to reappear in February and March 1919. In the worst week (that ending 2 November 1918) there were 262 deaths in the town from influenza and the pneumonia and bronchitis associated with it. All in all, these three outbreaks killed 1,600 people in Leicester. The disaster was widespread throughout Britain, and the world as a whole. The Local Government Board conducted an inquiry into it, in which Leicester was one of the towns selected for special study. At the end, the Medical Officer of Health candidly expressed his bewilderment: 'the investigation carried out in Leicester throws no light, unfortunately, on the mode in which the disease spreads. We are still in the dark as to this'. In some of its circumstances the epidemic recalled the plagues of the past. At one point the undertakers could not keep pace with the demands upon them, and the Corporation lent them the services of some of its employees; 100 coffins were made in the works of the Tramways Department.[2] Nothing like this had been experienced in Leicester since 1611. It was a dreadful visitation, in its timing and in itself.

A general election was held immediately the war was over. It was the first since 1910, and it took place under entirely new conditions imposed by the fourth Reform of Parliament, which had become law in June 1918. The electorate now included women aged thirty and more. Like nearly all other large towns, Leicester was divided into single-member constituencies. There were three of them, with boundaries corresponding to those of the County Borough since 1892. These changes did much to weaken the already declining Liberal party. To mention only

[1] *Ibid.*, 210–12, 271, 273.
[2] RMOH 1918, 9–12.

one reason – there were others, hardly less important[1] – it was plain that the addition of the well-to-do district of Stoneygate would greatly increase the Conservative vote in southern Leicester. The town now had the opportunity to express its opinion of MacDonald and his colleagues. It rejected them by enormous majorities, in favour of one Liberal and two Conservatives. MacDonald himself was defeated by more than three votes to one. Those who felt that he had cast a slur on the town could rejoice that it had now been removed. The explosion of feeling was what was to be expected. But it was sad, all the same. Whatever might be thought of MacDonald's pacifism, he had been a conscientious Member for twelve years; and he is the only man of high political distinction who has ever represented the borough in Parliament.

Five years later the town had the chance of securing a more illustrious Member, when Winston Churchill fought West Leicester as a Liberal against F. W. Pethick Lawrence. It was a noisy contest, which interested the whole country. For Churchill himself it was critical. Soundly defeated in Leicester and observing what had happened elsewhere, he came to the conclusion that Liberalism, even though the division between the followers of Asquith and Lloyd George had now been ended, was a spent force. He moved back to the Conservatives, won Epping at the next election, and stayed with Essex constituencies for the remainder of his political life. He took this defeat very hard and, magnanimous man though he was, never forgot it. Nearly thirty years afterwards, when he heard the town mentioned, he growled 'Beastly place, Leicester'.[2]

2

The four years' war completely stopped a number of developments that were on the way just before it began. The most important of them was in housing. By 1914 two things had become apparent. First, that houses were getting very scarce in the town: whereas at the beginning of 1911 over 1,300 had been vacant, by July 1914 there were virtually none. Second, that this was due at least in part to the reluctance of private builders to erect them, because the poorer tenants could not pay a rent that was economic. Municipalities had been authorised since 1890 to spend money from the rates on providing houses. Up to this point the Town Council of Leicester had not thought it necessary to do so. Now, however, it decided to act, and it directed its Estate Committee to prepare a scheme for the purpose. Exactly a week later war broke out, and all such plans had to be laid aside.[3]

[1] Clearly set out in VCHL iv. 242–3.
[2] H. Nicolson, *Diaries and Letters*, 1945–62 (Fontana edn), 175.
[3] Armitage, 5, 110, 219–20.

The situation was reviewed again in 1917, when the Estate Committee reported that at least 1,200 new houses would be needed at the end of the war and advised the Council that it should undertake to build some of them itself. In 1919 the Council took the first steps in this direction, when it bought two estates for the purpose, in Evington and Humberstone. Under the Housing Act of that year it went earnestly into the business. And indeed it was time. The number of houses required was stated now to have risen to 1,500; and even that may have been an under-estimate, for things were getting rapidly worse. In 1911 there had been 2,544 people in Leicester living more than two to a room; ten years later that number was 6,529 – even though the total of occupied dwellings had increased by 4·4 per cent. Nor was that merely a consequence of the social disturbances of the war, a reflection of a trend seen universally elsewhere. In Nottingham over the same years the number of people who lived in these conditions of overcrowding actually fell.[1]

The shortage of houses was not remedied quickly. The Corporation built about 750 in 1920–4, and a further 638 under the Housing Act of 1923. Two more estates were acquired to the south. But it was plain that this scale of operations was too small, and that the job could be done properly only if the Corporation would develop a really large site for the purpose. In the end it purchased the Braunstone estate, more than 1,000 acres in extent. Here was the start of a massive undertaking, which affected not only the city itself but also the county (cf. p. 125). Altogether, just over 9,000 houses were built by the Corporation in the years between the wars, and it assisted private builders to erect nearly 3,000 more.[2] This was now seen, moreover, as a continuing operation. In 1933–7 the Corporation went on to acquire the New Parks estate, though its development of that purchase was halted by the outbreak of the second German war.

The remarkable growth in house-building was not called for by any further significant increase of population. In the twenty years 1911–31 it rose by only 5·2 per cent (and, even so, that was more than in Nottingham, where the corresponding increase was 3·5). The explanation came from the accumulated overcrowding and from systematic slum clearance, which got under way in 1930, in terms of the Housing Act of that year. That meant the removal of many of the very poorest people in the city. Carried through on this scale, it opened up social and economic problems of an order never previously imagined. By 1939 a large part of St Margaret's parish had been cleared, making way for, among other things, a bus station and a municipal car park.

The mention of them indicates that we have now moved into a new age. Before the war motor vehicles had been a luxury. Now they became a normal part of daily life. The goods lorry rapidly drove out the horse and cart and destroyed the almost

[1] *Census of England and Wales, 1921: General Report* (1927), 53.
[2] The figures are in VCHL iv. 297–8.

complete monopoly the railway had come to exercise in the carriage of freight; the motor-bus began to eat up the railways' rural traffic and to challenge the tram in the towns; private motoring extended over the whole middle class, and beyond it – by 1930 a Morris Minor car cost only £100.

The motor-bus established itself firmly in Leicester in the 1920s. At first there were many rural services in the hands of very small operators, owning perhaps a single bus each – true successors to the nineteenth-century carriers, with their carts. Thus an uncle and nephew, Hylton and Dawson, set up a fourteen-seater bus about 1921 to ply between Glenfield and Leicester; the enterprise so founded, considerably enlarged, still exists – a most uncommon example – today.[1] Almost as soon as these small enterprises got going, however, the large company appeared beside them. Midland Red,[2] established in Birmingham and growing fast in that neighbourhood before the war, stretched out a long arm and began to operate from Leicester in 1922, setting up a garage for 100 buses there five years later.[3] That became the centre of a network of rural services, which gave many villages an ease of communication with the county town that they had never known before.

The Corporation, which had been slow to adopt the electric trams, was slow to abandon them too – though it was being urged to get rid of them at least as early as 1914.[4] It acquired its first motor-buses in 1924 and gradually extended their use: not, however, to replace the trams but to operate on new routes. In 1933 it considered, but rejected, the idea of substituting trolley-buses for trams. Four years later, however, it decided that the trams should gradually be removed, one route at a time, in favour of buses.[5] Northampton, Coventry, Derby, and Nottingham had all by then abandoned trams. Leicester became their last stronghold in the East Midlands.

When this decision was taken in 1937, it was primarily because the trams were alleged to obstruct traffic seriously in the centre of the town. That congestion, which had been worrying the City Council for a long time past, had other and more important causes. The chief of them lay in the plan of the streets themselves, and their narrow dimensions.

The street plan was an inheritance from the past. The medieval town could not be satisfactorily adapted to accommodate the traffic of the nineteenth century, still

[1] J. Wilshere, *Glenfield* [? 1971], 17.
[2] The Birmingham and Midland Motor Omnibus Company.
[3] J. Hibbs, *History of British Bus Services* (1968), 78.
[4] *Leicester Evening Post*, 31 August 1914.
[5] Pearson, *Leicester's Trams in Retrospect*, 48. There is a useful table, giving the precise dates of the extension of bus services, in *Public Transport in Leicester* (Leicester Museums, 1961), 27.

less that of the twentieth. The Clock Tower improvement of 1868, and the removal of the Wednesday Market from High Cross Street, shifted the traffic decisively to the east and south. The widened High Street was conceived as an artery for through traffic – and it was barely broad enough to take that from the start. The Clock Tower was the focus of the tramway system, of all the commercial and private traffic converging on the town, and of nearly all through traffic too.[1] Everything that travelled from London to Derby and Manchester by the road we now call A6 had to pass the Leicester Clock Tower.

Very early in the 'twenties the City Council addressed itself to this problem, and it came up with three solutions successively. The first was for a drastic and costly widening of Granby Street, Gallowtree Gate, and Belgrave Gate. It was soon abandoned in favour of the second, which provided for much less widening of existing streets and, instead, the cutting of new ones. This plan, put forward in 1924, was sufficiently radical to be described as 'a scheme to practically rebuild the town at a cost of £3 million'; it was to be carried through by stages, stretching over fifty years in all. It was strongly opposed, and rejected, though by no large majority, at a town's meeting.[2] The third plan then followed, and this was approved by the ratepayers and by Parliament in 1925: for the building of one new street, a broad thoroughfare to take the London–Manchester traffic away from the Clock Tower, with an associated widening of a short stretch of Belgrave Gate. The new road, Charles Street, was opened in some state by the Lord Mayor of London in 1932.

This plan did not stand alone. It was linked with others, to the same end. One-way traffic was introduced in 1926 along Belvoir Street, Bowling Green Street, and Pocklington's Walk. The first traffic lights appeared in the city in 1929 (Wolverhampton had been the pioneer in introducing them into the provinces, two years before). Though Charles Street was the only major new road actually built in these years, elaborate plans were adopted, for an inner ring road to encircle the city centre (with that street as one of its components) and for an outer road, at a radius of about three miles. Neither of these plans made any substantial progress at all, and the effect of that was doubly unsatisfactory. In the absence of these roads the traffic in the city grew steadily more intractable; and at the same time the uneasy knowledge of the possible construction of the roads some time in the future froze all enterprise that might lie in their path. Here, as in other ways, the want of forward, resolute planning can be seen as one of the cardinal failures of the 'twenties and 'thirties.

[1] There was one 'natural' by-pass, which an astute motorist could use if he wished, driving say from Coventry to Lincoln. He could avoid the Clock Tower by Fosse Road, Blackbird Road, and Abbey Park Road. How many people used it, one wonders?

[2] 126 *Builder* (1924) 101.

The chief blame for that ought not to rest, here at any rate, on the local authorities. The fault originated with the central Government and its first, disastrous incursion into town planning in 1909. The real effect of the Act passed then was not to promote town planning, but to impede it. The Corporation of Leicester was early in the field in preparing a scheme under the terms the Act laid down; but like almost every other body that made the same attempt, it found that the measure was 'a masterpiece of the obstructive art', and the plan it put forward was not realised.[1] Its next efforts, in the early 'twenties, were hampered by the ratepayers, who could quite fairly plead hard times and the very large new expenditure that was being incurred on housing. When the County Council initiated a general planning survey in 1930, the City cooperated; and the result, both as an analysis and as the statement of an agenda to the public, thoroughly justified itself.[2] One can detect very clearly at this time, and especially among some of the younger Labour members coming up on the City Council, an awareness of the necessity of planning comprehensively for the future, to seize chances that the new technologies were offering – and a frustration in the face of apathy and indifference.[3]

Though Charles Street is perhaps the most important memorial of these years, it is not the only one. The growth of municipal government compelled the Council to enlarge its accommodation. The Town Hall was extended at the back in 1924, in exact conformity with Hames's original building. Then, in 1938, it was supplemented by large new Municipal Offices in Charles Street. Perhaps the best that can be said of them, in architectural terms, is that they are of a piece with the street itself. They can give nobody any stirring of pleasure, as the Town Hall has done so constantly for 100 years. There are more satisfying buildings of this time: the Fire Station in Lancaster Road and its substantial housing, for example, by A. E. & T. Sawday, the Wyggeston Girls' School that faces it. Two notable branch libraries appeared away from the centre of the city, St Barnabas (1937) and Southfields (1939): an almost identical pair, each built round a low circular central hall, under the influence of Holden's distinguished Underground railway stations in London. The same architects, Symington Prince & Pike, were responsible for both the school and the libraries, in styles that are totally disparate.

But there is one other building of these years that towers over all the rest. No English town commemorated those who had served in the war more nobly than Leicester: for it consecrated to them a double monument, satisfactory in both its parts. The visual tribute was Lutyens's splendid War Memorial, unveiled in 1925: far seen from its commanding position on the lip of the valley to the south, the approaches to it enriched by the two sets of wrought-iron gates presented by

[1] Ensor, *England, 1870–1914*, 518.
[2] *Leicestershire Regional Planning Report* (1932).
[3] Reflected in Sir Charles Keene's interesting reminiscences (typescript in LRL).

Sir Jonathan North six years later and the delightful pavilions that flank them at the approach from the London Road. Lutyens's work, and the spirit that gave rise to it, happens to be unfashionable at the moment; but it rises high above the vagaries of fashion. It has the stuff of permanence. Leicester is fortunate indeed to have one of the finest works in England by the grand master of this kind of memorial. It resembles his larger work in Delhi, but on a careful scrutiny has been preferred to it.[1] Here, unexpectedly, Leicester leaps up out of its modest Midland valley, to present the northernmost monument in a unique series that stretches from India to South Africa and Picardy and England.

Nor was that all. To commemorate the suffering and sacrifice of the First World War, the people of Leicester and Leicestershire did more than erect a great war memorial. They founded a university.

3

The idea of establishing a university in Leicester had been brought forward more than once in the nineteenth century, in the wake of the achievements of Birmingham, Sheffield, and Nottingham.[2] But no citizen here took the lead with the generous idealism of Josiah Mason and Mark Firth. Nor was the Town Council willing to finance such a plan, as the Council did in Nottingham. The Council in Leicester had enough on its hands with the Colleges of Science and Art, in which it took a special and understandable pride. When the idea of a university did emerge effectively, it owed its initial impetus to an enthusiastic physician in the town, Dr Astley Clarke, with the steady support given to his plans by the Literary and Philosophical Society; and its fulfilment to the inspiration of making it a war memorial.

On this basis a subscription list was opened, at the time of the Armistice in 1918; an endowment fund was built up, which came to reach £103,000 by the end of 1920. Most of this money had come in moderate or small sums, though there were two large gifts of £20,000 each.[3] The biggest and most imaginative gift was not in cash but in kind. It was made by Thomas Fielding Johnson, a worsted-spinner, who silently purchased the disused buildings of the military hospital (formerly the Leicestershire and Rutland Lunatic Asylum), with the thirty-seven acres they stood in, for £40,000 and handed them over to serve the Wyggeston Boys' and Girls' Schools – both of which were in urgent need of re-housing at the time –

[1] A. S. G. Butler, *The Architecture of Sir Edwin Lutyens* (1950), iii. 40–1.
[2] Cf. Simmons, *New University*, chap. i.
[3] It was especially appropriate that one of these should have come from the hosiery industry (the sons of William Tyler), the other from the footwear manufacture (H. Simpson Gee).

together with the new College. By a happy and farsighted decision, his trustees reserved the building itself for the College, and it was wisely determined in the end that the site was not large enough to take all that the donor had designed, with the result that the girls came to be accommodated in 1926 in the new building, just mentioned, in Regent Road. The boys moved up in 1920: not indeed into any new structure, but into a miscellany of the outbuildings that had served the Asylum, and the hospital during the war. With its ample playing fields adjoining, the school was much more agreeably situated than it had been in the cramped and now very noisy quarters that the Trustees had erected for it in High Cross Street in 1877.

By contrast the University College was, at least potentially, accommodated in grandeur. Its late Georgian building of 1837, handled with an economical plainness and the unshakeable dignity of its tradition, was not indeed in very good repair, and funds for its maintenance were far from plentiful. But at least poverty prevented embellishment, which could hardly have failed, at that time, to be third-rate. Save only in one respect: in the good Leicester way, there were competent and tasteful gardeners among the members of the College Council, and they saw to it that the grounds were tended, so making possible the curved herbaceous border round the big front lawn that is perhaps the most pleasing physical distinction of the University today.

Only the front part of the building was commissioned to begin with, and that was brought into use gradually. The first students were admitted – nine of them – on 4 October 1921. Botany was the sole science taught at the outset, and when departments of chemistry and physics were added in 1925, a special public appeal had to be launched to endow and equip them. A generous burst of enthusiasm had founded the College. But most of those who had put their hands into their pockets in 1918–21 felt they had then done all that was needed. Like men who had provided the capital to house and set up a small business, they assumed it would now live on its own revenues: not indeed on its profits, but on the income from its endowment and from the fees of its students. That was quite impossible. Although fees came nearer then to covering the cost of educating students than they do now, they still fell far short of what was needed to make ends meet. There was no money whatever for even the most desirable development

How different that world was from ours! When the College began its work it did not draw a penny of its income from public funds. The City Council made its first contribution, of a farthing rate (then worth £1,140), in 1922–3. The County Council, which might have been expected to be no less concerned to foster the new institution, treated it with a studied chilliness that marked its contempt. Not until 1927 did it afford the smallest assistance; and then it tossed the College a derisory grant of £500 a year. This could be explained in part by the commitment the

County Council had accepted to develop a College of its own; a most enlightened and unusual idea, especially on the part of a local authority modest in size and wealth, which has fulfilled itself on a scale never imagined then as the Loughborough University of Technology. But there was more to it than that. The City and County had long looked askance at each other. In the nineteenth century they had nearly always differed in politics. The antagonism had become more evident, it had been institutionalised, after the passing of the Local Government Act of 1888, which set up a County Council with statutory powers, at some points rivalling the Town Council of Leicester. It is not perhaps surprising that the County Council should have regarded the College as the responsibility of the city: if Leicester wanted such an ostentatious piece of luxury, that was its business, and it must foot the bill. The notion of a joint enterprise, in any genuine sense, never arose.

But there was a further element too in the attitude of the County Council to the University College, less palpable though not perhaps less important. It was partly a matter of snobbery. Most Englishmen who thought about universities at all in these years — except those who lived in towns like Manchester or Leeds, with well-established civic universities of their own — thought of Oxford and Cambridge, with perhaps a vague notion that there was reputed also to be a university somewhere in London. When sons, or sometimes daughters, were in question, they would go to Oxford or Cambridge or (more probably) to no university at all. Whatever point could there be in setting up a tinpot College, lacking all the important social amenities, in an industrial town like Leicester?[1]

This type of reasoning had its counterpart, in other terms, in the city. There the common criticism the College had to meet arose from its failure to enter the field of applied science, from the stress it laid on the liberal, as against the useful, arts. That the College was an academic, not primarily a vocational institution, and that there were sound academic reasons for its policy could not be expected to weigh with those who were not themselves academically minded. What they saw was a new institution that diverted young men from business or a profession when they left school and occupied them for three years with matters that seemed to bear not at all on the way in which they were afterwards to earn their living. Again, what good purpose was served by that? Far better, surely, to put any money that might be available for higher education into practical training, which was already furnished by the municipal Colleges of Science and Art.

Such arguments as these were by no means peculiar to Leicester. But they

---

[1] One other thing also contributed to the distaste felt by some County Councillors for the College. Its first Principal, R. F. Rattray, was a vehement and outspoken opponent of blood-sports; an attitude that could hardly be expected to commend him or his institution in Leicestershire.

operated there with a special force because the University College, round which they revolved, was so vulnerable to them. It lacked prominent, wealthy, and vocal supporters, whether on the City Council or in private life. Its work was a perpetual grinding struggle, with ludicrously inadequate funds, in a community that was generally either hostile or indifferent. The College did not lack friends, and good ones, who quietly helped to keep it going in times of difficulty. Its first two Principals, R. F. Rattray and F. L. Attenborough, held on their way with admirable tenacity, refusing to be discouraged in circumstances that would have driven many men in their position to despair. Good work, when judged by high academic standards, was performed by some of the College's students; the general body of them built up a sound corporate tradition that engendered respect. It grew as a cooperative enterprise, out of the public eye.

This part of Leicester's memorial to the First World War was founded in a mood of special emotion, with an enthusiasm that soon cooled. In the years between the Wars — as one of its distinguished students, Professor J. H. Plumb, observed recently — it was 'the sickly child of a few dedicated and determined citizens and town councillors, and it impinged scarcely at all on city life'.[1] In the long run, however, the College advanced and justified itself, though some of the directions it came to take were very different from any that had been contemplated in 1918.

If the University College was the most important new educational development of these years in the city, it was not the only one. The Gateway School, founded in 1928, was in some ways a pioneer enterprise, designed to provide secondary education for boys intending to work in the local industries. Hitherto, they had had to look for much of their training to the junior departments of the Colleges of Science and Art. Now, at the age of eleven, they could be taken into this school, which collaborated closely with the adjoining Colleges but developed quite separately to meet the needs of these boys. It started with 270 of them; by 1939 there were 430.

The senior grammar schools in the city continued to grow (the Wyggeston Boys' School reached a peak of 1,004 in 1929), and they overcame in large measure the drawbacks that their chequered history had imposed on them. Apart from the Wyggeston Girls' School, none of them was handsomely housed. Though the Wyggeston Boys' School got some new buildings, the chief of which was an assembly hall, it was accommodated largely in the Nissen huts that had been erected as an extension of the old military hospital. This was understandable in the immediate aftermath of the war, when it would have been impossible to provide new buildings. What was disappointing, and ultimately became a scandal to the city,

[1] LM 4 November 1971: University Golden Jubilee Supplement.

was that the School continued to occupy these makeshift quarters for a whole generation to come.

4

The years between the wars present a curious phase in the history of Leicester. In pure externals, the town advanced in consideration. On 10 June 1919 George V came down with Queen Mary, making the first formal visit paid by a sovereign for nearly 300 years and knighting Jonathan North in the De Montfort Hall. In the following month the appellation 'County Borough' was changed to 'City'. Nine years later the title of the first citizen became 'Lord Mayor'. In the meantime Cyril Bardsley, the energetic Bishop of Peterborough, had procured the division of his see into two, with the western part based upon Leicester. In token of his entire belief in the wisdom of this measure, he himself in a sense stepped down, to become the first bishop of the new diocese in 1926. St Martin's was chosen as the cathedral church.

Only the last of these changes was of more than formal significance. An austere observer might smile at them a little sardonically. For they were not compliments paid to a town leaping forward in size and power, nor to one that had distinguished itself recently in solving its own moral and material problems. Such compliments might have been timely in the 'eighties. Now they had only an empty meaning. Almost all English towns larger than Leicester, and some that were smaller, enjoyed these distinctions already: so Leicester was entitled to them, as a formality, too.

That austere observer might go on to point out that at the time when they were bestowed, the city's abounding growth had virtually ceased and that it displayed some of the signs of stagnation, even of retrogression. The oldest Leicester newspaper, the *Journal* of 1753, closed down in 1920. The city's one morning paper the *Daily Post*, was discontinued in the following year, and replaced by the *Evening Mail*. At the same time the old *Mercury* was reorganised. Henceforward there were two daily papers only, both published in the evening. They were healthy competitors on occasion (and the historian must be grateful to them still); but neither one nor the two together could be a substitute for the newspaper on the Victorian breakfast table, which presented local news and opinion, side by side with national, in close relationship, and could comment on it all with a mature deliberation to be achieved only by a paper produced overnight.

For the rest, the theatre remained flaccid. The city had an outstanding concert hall, but very few concerts. With the death of Perkins Pick (who had been a

Vice-President of the R.I.B.A.) in 1919 the succession of notable Leicester architects was broken.[1]

If these were all losses of one kind, how much can we see to compensate for them in other directions? A little perhaps, not much. The city paid greater attention to its antiquities than the Victorian town had done. The Corporation lavished care and money on restoring the old Guildhall, which was reopened by a celebrated and rather depressing figure of that time, Dean Inge, in 1926.[2] In 1935, having determined to build new swimming baths immediately to the west of the Jewry Wall, it agreed to allow the site to be thoroughly investigated by a well-qualified archaeologist, in the expectation that this would reveal the Roman Forum. Dr Kathleen Kenyon undertook the task. It soon appeared that the Romans had anticipated the Corporation of Leicester by laying out baths there, and that the site was indeed of great interest. So much so that the Corporation agreed to build its baths elsewhere, to allow the investigation to be prolonged through four seasons, and at the end to keep the site permanently open. This was a really enlightened decision, much assailed by the ignorant. To the Victorian Town Council it would have been unthinkable.

The City Museum had been lifted well above its modest beginnings – largely through the work of two distinguished Curators, Montagu Browne and E. E. Lowe – to become recognised as one of the most progressive municipal enterprises of its kind in the country. In the 'twenties its work began to be extended into the schools. It was one of the first provincial museums to employ a guide-lecturer for the purpose, from 1924; ratepayers' money began to be spent even on the purchase of specimens required solely for educational use.[3] At this time too the Museum's responsibilities extended, by the acquisition of the Newarke Houses, and of the delightful Belgrave Hall in 1936.

The city still lacked an art gallery. It had a sizeable collection of indifferent paintings, mostly Victorian, and a few good ones,[4] housed in the Museum in New

---

[1] There are two outstandingly good obituaries of Pick, by A. Hamilton Thompson in 11 TLAS (1920) 401–5 and by S. H. Skillington in Leicester Society of Architects, 46 *Report* 18–21. The latter includes the delicious comment – characteristic of its author – that Pick had 'a wholesome contempt for the spurious antique and for unpedigreed novelty'.

[2] The restoration of the building is illustrated in a series of measured drawings in 13 TLAS (1923–4), following p. 72.

[3] *Leicester Museum and the Schools* (1934), 2.

[4] In old age G. F. Watts presented an early painting, *Fata Morgana*, which he himself described as 'one of my best works', to the Corporation to encourage it to form an art gallery. He was moved to do so by admiration for 'the service your townsman Mr John M. Cook [Thomas Cook's son] is rendering, especially in Egypt, to the nation, making its name respected by admirable administration and fair dealing': 58 *Builder* (1890) 50.

Walk. Some effort was made to improve and extend the collection in these years, chiefly through the efforts of Alderman Charles Squire (the only layman who has ever served as President of the Museums Association). This might be seen at least as a declaration of intent.

One other amenity was acquired by the citizens at this moment. They had long regarded Bradgate Park with a special affection, pouring out there at holiday times, or whenever they had the opportunity throughout the year. Though some people might feel more drawn to the landscape of East Leicestershire, that was hedged and ditched everywhere, whilst Bradgate was open, high, good for walking, for picnics, or just gently taking the air. The Grey family were now disposed to part with it, and it passed into the hands of the City and County Councils jointly in 1928. They were enabled to acquire it through the munificence of Charles Bennion, Chairman of the British United Shoe Machinery Company, who bought the estate and made it over to them. A body of trustees was set up to manage the Park, which thus became the permanent possession of the whole community. The matter was settled amicably between the two local government authorities; they both took pleasure and pride in the acquisition. Joint action between them was never easy to achieve, and in some ways was becoming more difficult. Such close collaboration as this was an encouraging sign for the future.

Bradgate now became, as a matter of right and not of grace, the chief playground of Leicester, accessible at week-ends cheaply and with ease. The full summer holiday continued, and was steadily developed, to a pattern established in the Victorian age. The economic life of the city was interrupted – though not totally suspended – at the beginning of August to permit the workers and their families to stream out by rail to the sea. Some fifty special trains were run for this purpose, by the London Midland & Scottish Railway alone, in 1939 – laborious affairs, for most of them were worked by goods engines, by no means of the newest, from Nuneaton.[1] Allowing for the passengers carried by the rival company, the London & North Eastern, which had in its hands the traffic to Skegness and Cleethorpes, and for those who went by ordinary trains, it seems safe to say that at least 50,000 people – a fifth of the whole population – must have left Leicester by train on those Bank Holiday week-ends.

5

A good many writers, of one sort and another, recorded their impressions of Leicester in these years. Few strangers gave it more than tepid approval; some a good deal less than that. Mr Justice Mackinnon, for example (no ordinary Judge;

[1] J. M. Dunn, *Reflections on a Railway Career* (1966), 111.

the editor of Fanny Burney's *Evelina*), found 'little left of antiquity or picturesqueness in the city', and though he appreciated Belgrave Hall and House, saw everything around as 'a waste of dinginess' and wrote off the Jewry Wall with a rather ill-informed disdain. He was pleased, however, to light on a good second-hand bookshop.[1] (Which was it, one wonders? In those happy days there were two.) To Harold Nicolson, who represented the West constituency in Parliament from 1935 to 1945, Leicester was no more than 'that ugly and featureless city'.[2] J. B. Priestley found it featureless too. 'There are many worse places I would rather live in', he wrote in 1934. 'It seemed to me to lack character, to be busy and cheerful and industrial and built of red brick, and to be nothing else.' However, when he went out to lunch in a house of the 'nineties in Stoneygate he allowed that it was a good one and gave credit to the town's craftsmen and designers, whose praise he had heard sung before.[3]

Such impressions as these were, in general, endorsed by judicious and perceptive citizens. They thought Leicester a pleasant place to live in, with its ample open spaces, well-tended gardens and trees, the freedom from obvious dirt in its atmosphere. But though they found it comfortable, they also – just like Nevinson in the 1860s – were apt to find it uninspiring and dull. If they wanted excitement, something a little heady and brash, they went to find it in Nottingham.

All this is reflected, clearly and well, in fiction. Neither Leicester nor its county threw up an Arnold Bennett or a D. H. Lawrence. There is nothing for Leicester to be compared with the portrait of Nottingham in the works of Alan Sillitoe. Yet Leicester bore and bred C. P. Snow, and two of his Lewis Eliot novels are set there almost entirely, *Strangers and Brothers* and *Time of Hope*.[4] More recently, William Cooper (H. S. Hoff) set two novels there, *Scenes from Provincial Life* (1950) and *Young People* (1958). Both these writers describe it at first hand, from their recollections of Alderman Newton's School and the infant University College in the 'twenties and 'thirties.

Nowhere in those four novels is there any extended attempt to depict the city. The powerful quality of the Potteries forces itself into the mind, the eyes and nostrils, of every reader of Arnold Bennett; for many people the Five Towns are the greatest characters in his books. Here, in these novels of our own time, Leicester is hardly more than the faintly-indicated background against which their wry comedies are played. Would any of these stories be much different, one may

[1] F. D. Mackinnon, *On Circuit* (1940), 205.
[2] *Diaries and Letters*, 1945–62, 243.
[3] *English Journey* (1934), 119, 126–8.
[4] They were published in that order, in 1940 and 1949 respectively. But the later novel reaches back further in time. It begins in 1914, *Strangers and Brothers* in 1925.

ask, if they had worked themselves out in the same social milieu in Derby or Wolverhampton?

It would be wrong to say no, and simple-minded too. If Leicester does not pervade these books with the pungent reek of the Five Towns, that is because Leicester is itself without pungency. These writers are interested in people, hardly at all in places: in this respect they stand wholly outside the tradition of Dickens and Hardy. Yet their presentation of Leicester, within the narrow limits deliberately chosen for it, is sharp, unmistakable, and entirely authentic: of the Town Hall Square,[1] of Pocklington's Walk and the Leicestershire Club,[2] of the richly fragrant – and now vanished – Mikado Café in the Market Place,[3] of Alderman Newton's Boys' School and the Central Lending Library.[4] Here is the Clock Tower, perfectly hit off through the confused minds of the townspeople:

> Our clock-tower did provoke wonder. Its ugliness set fire to the imagination, but that was only the beginning of wonderment. In the first place I always used to wonder why anybody had ever put it there. For displaying the time of day it was totally unnecessary: the surrounding shop-fronts were plastered with an assortment of clocks which offered the public the widest choice in times they could possibly have wished for. Could it be, I wondered as I stared at its majestic erectness, our contribution to the psychopathology of everyday life? And who had designed it? Was such a monument designed by an architect who specialised for life on clock-towers; or was it thrown off by some greater man in his hour of ease? Surely the latter! Small wonder, then, that the citizens of our town were proud of the clock-tower. It had its place in our hearts. 'It's ugly', we thought, 'but it's home!'[5]

Above all, with a sure instinct, both novelists fasten on the New Walk: not the lower end, with its elegant small houses, already beginning then to go down hill, but Upper New Walk, ostentatious in its late Victorian manner and also undergoing a subtle change in character:

> I walked to Morcom's flat in the early evening. The way led from the centre of the town, and suddenly took one between box-hedges and five-storey, gabled, Victorian houses, whose red brick flared in the sunset with a grotesque and Gothic cosiness. But the cosiness vanished, when one saw their dark windows: once, when the town was smaller, they had been real houses: now they were offices, shut for the night. Only Martineau's, at the end of the Walk, remained a

[1] C. P. Snow, *Time of Hope* (1951 edn.), 66, 97.
[2] *Ibid.*, 106–7.
[3] *Ibid.*, 223; W. Cooper, *Scenes from Provincial Life* (1950), 11.
[4] *Ibid.*, 34–5, 217.
[5] *Ibid.*, 251.

solid private house. The one next door, which he also owned, had been turned into flats: and there Morcom lived, on the top floor.[1]

When the Upper New Walk appears in *Young People*, it is with the percipient comment that its houses had originally been occupied by prosperous boot-manufacturers, who divided their lives between these houses, their offices and works, and the Wesleyan chapels. 'But they had long since taken themselves off to one of the suburbs, to bigger, if less substantial houses, with gardens all round them and a golf course near by – chapel-going had been allowed to slide.'[2] There is one of the chief facts of Leicester's social and economic history in the twentieth century. Just as in the nineteenth century the prosperous business men had moved out from the old town, low flying and unhealthy, to the higher ground and especially to Stoneygate, so in the twentieth they were moving out of Leicester altogether, beyond the suburbs even, to live in Charnwood Forest or at places like Horninghold, whence they could come into town daily with ease in half an hour's driving by motor-car or less.

To a city still dominated by the family business, this mattered very much indeed, depriving it of the leadership that public-spirited citizens, resident in the place, had given it in earlier days. There were no more Biggses or Israel Harts. The last of that line was Sir Jonathan North.

6

The Second World War affected Leicester very differently from the First.

For one thing, the city suffered physical damage. The first air-raid occurred on the morning of 21 August 1940. The targets were presumably the gas works and the power station; the bombs fell just south of them and killed six people. Other raids followed, on a small scale, in the autumn. The heaviest attack came on 19 November, causing scattered damage over a large tract of the city, east and south of the Old Town. It was greatest in the Highfields, and there the worst single disaster occurred, at the corner of Tichborne Street and Highfield Street, where forty-one people were killed. There was also substantial damage in Stoneygate. The Town Hall had a narrow escape, when a high-explosive bomb fell through the roof and failed to go off. Freeman Hardy & Willis's premises were destroyed in Rutland Street. On the next night a parachute mine demolished the Pavilion (the old grand-stand of the racecourse) on the Victoria Park.

That was, in effect, all. A total of 122 people were killed in the city, first and last; 255 houses were destroyed, fifty-six factories, and one school. The people did

[1] C. P. Snow, *Strangers and Brothers* (1951 edn.), 26.
[2] W. Cooper, *Young People* (1958), 7.

their best to make light of the whole business. Harold Nicolson, going down to visit his constituents after the chief raid, reported that they seemed 'amused more than anything else'.[1] But that was taking it a shade too easily. Leicester never suffered any concentrated attack, like those on Coventry and Birmingham; there were no raids whatever, even minor ones, after 13 July 1941. In that sense the city was immeasurably fortunate. Nevertheless, this was the first time it had seen or heard anything of warfare since 1645.[2]

Economic and social life was much more minutely regulated than it had been in 1914–18. Rationing was no matter for any local committee to improvise. It was imposed by the Government, and came to extend to almost every article of life. Since conscription was decreed from the outset, there was no argument about recruiting. The casualty lists were shorter and did not have the same numbing, obsessive effect as before. Yet the total weariness that the war induced was scarcely less. The fighting lasted eighteen months longer; and well before its conclusion it was plain that the part played by the country in the life of the world was diminishing in importance. So many of the expectations of 1918 had proved delusive. With that experience behind, the future looked drab indeed in 1945.

Drab, and highly bewildering. The war had wrought great changes in the city's economy. The policy of industrial concentration imposed by the Government, grouping firms and their production together, in order to provide factory space and release manpower for making armaments, was applied to the hosiery manufacture first of all. Before long it was extended to the footwear industry too. This produced much dislocation in the established trades, if also a measure of involuntary rationalisation. Both industries flourished in terms of production, within the limits imposed on them; but nobody could predict what their condition and prospects would be like when the special circumstances of the war had passed. Meanwhile, one thing was quite clear: that, in consequence of these measures, the engineering trades had come to play a much more important part in the economy of Leicester than they had ever done in the past. Would this continue? Would the new firms that had arrived in Leicester to undertake work connected with the war remain behind? And, if so, how were the older-established industries going to fare in competition for the labour they needed?

These questions, and many more, posed themselves insistently in 1945. The answers to them had to be worked out against the shifting background of a novel and complex world.

[1] *Diaries and Letters,* 1939–45, 126.
[2] Cf. *Leicester Blitz Souvenir* (n.d.).

III
Yesterday and Today

———

The history of Leicester is a very even story, seldom broken by violent change, political, economic, or social. At one point in the past it is perhaps allowable to say that something like a revolution occurred in the town's affairs – in the Mid-Victorian age, roughly between 1860 and 1880. It seems clear that we are now living through another revolution, a hundred years afterwards.

Far-reaching changes were foreshadowed at the close of the war in 1945. They began to take effect in the 1950s. In the 'sixties the pace grew steadily quicker. The trot became a canter about 1970; at the moment it looks almost like a gallop. Many aspects of life in Leicester continue as they have done for a long time past. But physically the city is going through what can certainly be called, without any stretching of language, a revolution; and that reflects in some measure a series of social changes, which in turn it helps to further.

This chapter and the next attempt to marshal some of the outstanding elements in this process, to set them in order and estimate their significance. But it has all to be seen against the background of what does not change, or changes only very slowly: since continuity has been, for centuries past, a powerful ingredient in the mixture of which Leicester is constituted, and it is so still.

Let us begin by surveying the city proper, as we have considered it historically, within its statutory boundaries. Then, in the next chapter, we can move on to examine an entity that has emerged only within the last hundred years and is still imperfectly defined: the urban complex that we are coming now to describe as Greater Leicester.

I

An emigrant, who left Leicester at the close of the Second World War and returned there for the first time today, might find things superficially little altered. If he arrived at the station and made for the Clock Tower he would note, with pleasure or sentimental regret, the disappearance of the trams. (The last of them ran in 1949.) Moving down Granby Street, he might observe some new concrete buildings on the left; but the Grand Hotel is still there at present, not a pinnacle changed, and the Midland Bank stands out, more prominently than before, handsomely bizarre in its cleaned vermilion brick. He would find the pedestrian respected in Gallowtree Gate, and Adderly's (or Marshall & Snelgrove's) gone. As for the Clock Tower, he could greet it still as an old friend, entirely unchanged in itself though no longer dominating its environment; crouching rather, in some apprehension, beneath the concrete cliff of Littlewood's (Plate 16b). And if he then glanced along the roads that radiate outwards from this point, he would probably continue to think that not much had changed. He might miss the small hotels – the George submerged, the White Hart and the Stag and Pheasant, with their warm hospitable grill-rooms, vanished. He would certainly miss the Bell in Humberstone Gate and observe the huge Haymarket Centre that occupies its site. But elsewhere things would be as he remembered them: St Mark's spire rising up in Belgrave Gate and the Cathedral's above Silver Street; the High Street as straight and drab as ever; Churchgate, with its delectably sinuous course, framing the tower of St Margaret's at the northern end.

If he wandered further through the Old Town, however, he would soon discover that that last streetscape is now unique. Another that he might recall, that of High Cross Street, has been dismembered; and that is a serious loss, for it was, both visually and historically, the most remarkable street in Leicester.

The centre of the city has been at the Clock Tower only since 1868. The historic centre is at the junction of High Cross Street and High Street, where the High Cross itself stood, marking the point fairly and squarely like Carfax at Oxford and the Cross at Gloucester. If our visitor went to look for the site of the High Cross now, he would indeed be able to find it, but no longer corresponding to that description. For the southern part of High Cross Street has been subsumed into a new roadway called St Nicholas Circle, and the site of the Cross is therefore no longer at the meeting-point of four roads.[1] Standing there now, he would

[1] The last fragment of the Cross itself was taken away in 1836. But its exact position was marked in the surface of High Cross Street by stones set in the form of a cross; and with commendable piety this has been preserved. It is the one surviving memorial of the ancient centre of Leicester.

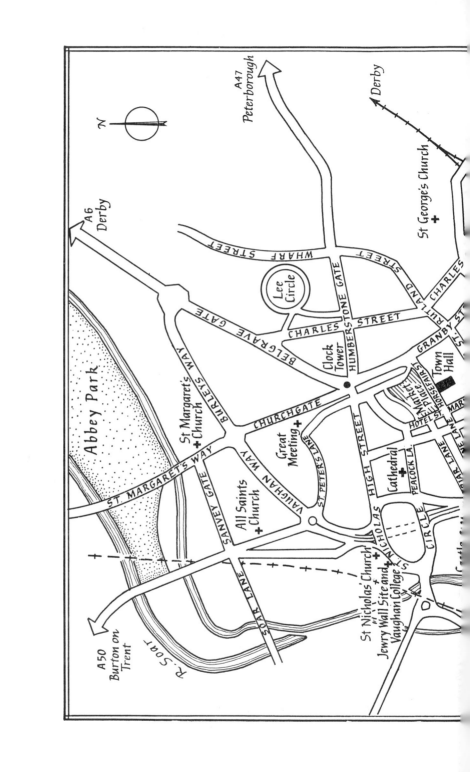

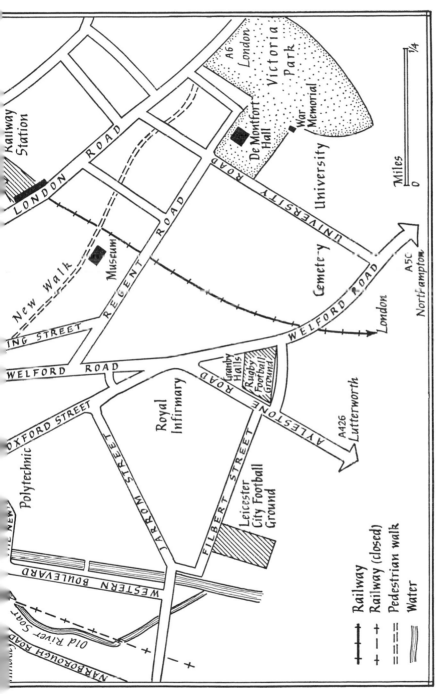

Central Leicester in 1974

witness the great changes that have been under way throughout the past ten years. The new road system sweeps traffic rapidly round from east and west through St Nicholas Circle into Red Cross Street beyond. High Cross Street is now truncated. All that survives of it in recognisable form is part of the northern section, and that is a sad spectacle to anybody who knew it only ten or fifteen years ago. For this street kept until lately a contour and character all its own. It made its way northwards, to the North Gate of the medieval town, in a fairly direct course. But there was a wavering irregularity in the building line, accentuated by the projection of All Saints church into the roadway, that made it a delightful piece of ancient townscape; one of the most subtly pleasing things in the whole city. All this was ruthlessly destroyed when Vaughan Way was built, with a large roundabout sitting plum in the middle of High Cross Street, breaking its continuity beyond repair.

That was grievous. Yet one must admit that it would be hard to justify the large expense that would have had to be incurred to avoid this destruction, the expense of building an underpass. High Cross Street is not today a prosperous thoroughfare, full of wealthy shops. It is an irrelevant inconvenience in a town of the twentieth century: narrow and impracticable for motor traffic, its buildings decayed and yet scarcely distinguished enough to merit restoration. If the Wyggeston Boys' School had so little sense of its past as to allow its original building to remain a carpet warehouse and then to be turned into the offices of a bus company, can we expect enlightenment anywhere else?

In the course of the last fifteen years – no more – the Old Town of Leicester has been almost entirely destroyed. In the late 1950s its medieval street plan was clearly visible, and it was dominated by the industrial buildings that summarised and embodied the town's Victorian prosperity. Now nearly all this has gone: not merely the streets but their very names – Applegate Street, Blue Boar Lane, Bakehouse Lane, Red Cross Street;[1] and almost all the chief commercial buildings, notably Everard's Brewery at the top of Castle Street and Preston's boot factory, with its double-curved front, in Bakehouse Lane. In their place we have a huge swath of concrete, taking the traffic through the city north and south, with windy and desolate stretches, of concrete again, on either side of it. The Old Town in its former state was grimy, and in many respects an inefficient anachronism. Never-

---

[1] One or two praiseworthy attempts have been made to perpetuate the tradition of the old names, but they have sometimes falsified history. 'Southgates', for example, is a misnomer, arising from the modern failure to understand the Danish use of 'gate' for 'street' in Leicester (i.14). 'Gates' was a term used exclusively for the site of the gates themselves; it is correctly preserved in 'East Gates'. And the Haymarket development has assumed a quite wrong name. The Hay Market was on the other side of the Clock Tower. Accuracy matters here: there is no point in preserving an old name if it is to be applied to a different site 100 yards and more away.

theless it was full of interest, of oddity; it was lovable and contained surprises. Not one of those things is true of its successor. It has become a passage-way, a mere hyphen between larger units. Can anybody feel the smallest interest in such a place?

But of course there is much more to be said, on the other side. A passage-way through the city for the northbound traffic had got to be forced, all the more urgently after the opening of the neighbouring section of the M1 in 1965. It has been forced effectively by this road, by Vaughan Way, and by St Margaret's Way. Access to the motorway, both north and south, still has its points of inconvenience; but these big road works have immensely relieved the worst congestion, towards the centre of the city. It must be recognised too that St Nicholas Circle, with the American-owned Holiday Inn at its centre, straddling the new road underpass, is a bold and clear-cut piece of engineering. It has wrenched the heart out of the Old Town – the tract between the Romans' Forum and the Normans' Castle; but it has done so in a way that would have excited the admiration of both those hard-headed peoples. It has created a new kind of symmetry, which could yet be made to yield a striking final achievement.

Three monuments of the ancient world survive here, very firmly protected now from injury or destruction. The appearance of two of them, the Jewry Wall and St Nicholas church, has been greatly enhanced by the erection of the new Vaughan College and Museum to face them. The third, the house that has become the Museum of Costume, is a building of high interest, which has been preserved from destruction against heavy odds, to the credit of the Corporation.[1] These buildings do not sit happily, environed in concrete; the Newarke gateway to the south (now the Museum of the Leicestershire Regiment) is grossly insulted by its surroundings.[2] But they are the enduring signs of the quite different world that the twentieth century has overlaid. By accepting the construction of the large hotel and the adjoining offices the city has declared that this is to be a place of settlement as well as a set of traffic junctions. Is it to remain something ordinary, of the kind we are only too familiar with, for example in the City of London – a haphazard conjunction of the ancient and the entirely new? Or can St Nicholas Circle become, in the French sense, a *Place* of a quite new kind, belonging entirely to the motor age and yet affording piquant interest and even repose to human beings? The thing is still possible, under firm planning touched with imagination. But the hour is very late;

[1] To keep the record straight, it should be noted that the house owes its preservation chiefly to the signal pertinacity of Mr T. A. Walden, Director then of Museums in Leicester and now in Glasgow.

[2] More grossly than is in any way necessary. If the repulsive fibre-glass pyramids beside it were removed, in favour of conventional and inconspicuous skylights to illuminate the passage below, the evil would be markedly reduced.

and the hideous signs that the Holiday Inn has been permitted to erect cannot inspire one with the confidence one would wish to feel in the result.

A City Councillor of Leicester, responsible for its economical and orderly government – or indeed any good citizen – may well feel that the demands of our world are of infinitely greater importance than the preservation of the past. The historian must recognise that if there is a conflict the living will prevail over the dead. But need there always be conflict? Can we not recognise that in this city, in our age, material needs have already prevailed absolutely and that no one doubts they will continue to do so; but that there are also things of the spirit, and that in some of them Leicester is exceptionally endowed? 'In no town', an antiquary observed sixty years ago, 'is the position of the [Roman and medieval] walls more clearly marked out by the planning of the streets'.[1] That remark, surprisingly, holds good today. Would any intelligent person doubt that it should be borne in mind when further changes in the alignment of streets are laid down? 'The group of Castle, St Mary, the Newarke, St Nicholas, the Roman Baths, St Martin, and the Guildhall is something the patriotic citizen of Leicester might proudly take any visitor to, British or foreign': the words are Sir Nikolaus Pevsner's, published in 1960.[2] Those buildings are all still there, but they no longer exist now as a group: the new road system has ripped them apart. Can we not profit by that grim example and conserve carefully and sympathetically what remains to us, while there is still time?

St Nicholas Circle is not yet complete. The roadway is to be widened on its eastern side when the buildings of Alderman Newton's Boys' School (the Wyggeston School of 1877) can be vacated. That will enable the Cathedral and the Guildhall to be linked visually with the other old buildings, and help to create a fresh unity of its own. But one most important unity is emphatically lacking now and seems to be inadequately provided for in the future. The whole of this development has been dictated by the motor-car; and in the course of realising it the pedestrian, the independent human being, has been at some points almost forgotten. A visitor – most appropriately perhaps, an American – drives himself into the Holiday Inn, eats his dinner, looks out of a window to the north, sees a flood-lit church close by, and strolls out to investigate. How does he get across the road, with the traffic racing up the hill from the West Bridge to Vaughan Way? If he is prepared to wait, and is then bold and nimble, he can do it. Otherwise he probably abandons the attempt – and so misses one of the striking sights of Leicester. There is a foot-bridge spanning the whole of St Nicholas Circle, but the access to it is ingeniously concealed. He is in effect a prisoner on an island, and he can get out of it with safety only in a machine, even in order to reach a point less than 100 yards

[1] A. Harvey, *The Castles and Walled Towns of England* (1911), 224.
[2] *The Buildings of England: Leicestershire and Rutland*, 136.

away. What is to be thought of the city, when it takes so much trouble to illuminate and display its monuments, yet renders them inaccessible to just the kind of visitors who might be expected to appreciate them most highly?

All in all, the development of St Nicholas Circle is an interesting spectacle. It could in the end turn out to be something of a triumph, or a shabby failure, or a mixture of both.

In three respects the buildings that are now going up in Leicester are totally different from those of the past: in scale, in material and colour. The tall building has become a commonplace here, as elsewhere in Britain, only within the last ten years, with its logical accompaniment, the four or six-lane street. And concrete has replaced brick as the prevailing material. The red and green town of the Victorian age (pp. 47–8) survived until 1945. Now it has largely disappeared in favour of one showing a series of tones of dirty buff. There is no longer any contrast between the body of a building and its roof: so the element of variety afforded even by the dull Welsh slate has gone. Concrete *can* be handled with sensibility; or *can* be faced with another material to hide it. Both these measures are expensive and therefore uncommon. A 'prestige' office building, in the absurd vocabulary of our time, means only one that is high or conspicuous, not one that is elegant, outside or in. Many architectural moralists of today disapprove of a facing designed to disguise concrete or steel or common brick, quite as primly as their Victorian predecessors disapproved of stucco. But, just as we may feel that those Victorian moralists were often (though not always) wrong, we should surely be prepared to recognise that faced buildings may often succeed: the Royal Insurance Building, for instance, in Charles Street (by Pick Everard Keay & Gimson, 1966); the tower of the University's Engineering Building, faced with tiles from Holland, in the then rare and unfashionable colour of red (Stirling & Gowan, 1962).[1]

It cannot, alas, be contended that much of the new building in the city shows distinction, or even affords a moment of pleasurable surprise. When Sir Nikolaus Pevsner cast his eye over Leicester, in the late 1950s, he found nothing recent that he could praise at all except a single house in Avenue Road. The most he could say was that the University had chosen Sir Leslie Martin as its consultant architect, in a scheme of development then getting under way, and that therefore his 'hope for the future and a true twentieth-century Leicester [was] . . . focussed on that quarter'.[2] If he were to return to examine Leicester now, fifteen years later, he would certainly find more to discuss and criticise, though in proportion to the mass

[1] A welcome tendency to return to red brick has become apparent very lately: in the new Haymarket Centre, for example, and in a number of small office buildings in Friar Lane and Millstone Lane.

[2] *The Buildings of England: Leicestershire and Rutland*, 41, 137, 164.

of building that has gone up during those years, the amount that would be worth his attention would not be large.

To begin where Sir Nikolaus broke off, at the University. One part of its site, then entirely virgin, has now been completely occupied with buildings laid out according to Sir Leslie Martin's dispositions and – with one exception, the Adrian Building for the biological sciences – harmonising well together. For that exception he was in no way to blame: it transgressed, in scale and in colour, all the principles that ruled everywhere else on the site. But for that one mistake, Leicester might have had a complex of buildings as entirely coherent as those, say, of New College at Oxford, reflecting in their own way the prevailing intellectual interests of the 1960s as surely as New College reflects those of the 1380s.[1] For the rest, the University's new buildings must be seen as single units. One – the Engineering Building, just mentioned – has achieved an international reputation, which may well last.[2] The tallest and thickest of them, the Attenborough Building, stands forward, in a domineering position at the very top of the slope the University occupies. Through the wise insistence of the city's planners and of Sir Leslie Martin, however, tall buildings have been kept well away from Lutyens's War Memorial, which continues to exercise its own serene domination.

No other group of recently-erected buildings in Leicester has the same interest. But the University is by no means the only institute of higher education in the city, and two others have also made distinctive contributions to the same end. The City of Leicester College of Education has successfully developed a charming site at Scraptoft – beyond the city boundary, but well within Greater Leicester – with buildings that are modest in scale and skilfully disposed, to a plan by Messrs Bridgwater & Shepheard. The estate, with its delightful manor house of 1723 (see Plates 17b, 22b), was bought by the Corporation in 1954; the first group of new buildings was completed in 1960. The municipal Colleges of Art and Technology were translated into a Polytechnic in 1969. Radiating out from Perkins Pick's building of 1897 (see p. 26), the Polytechnic is coming to occupy a whole quarter of the city, including a small fragment of the Old Town, stretching south and west from the Newarke to the river, to displace a large tract of little houses in decay. Its buildings have been designed in the City Architect's Department. The most conspicuous of them is the James Went Building, with its slit windows irregularly spaced. It occupies part of the Newarke and challenges the spire of St

---

[1] Any comparison of aesthetic merit would be absurd. If somebody attempted so unprofitable a task, he would have to begin by noticing the total disappearance – one might almost say the supersession – of craftsmanship in the twentieth-century buildings: something highly characteristic of our time.

[2] Cf. for example P. Kidson *et al.*, *History of English Architecture* (Pelican edn., 1965), 320; D. Stephen *et al.*, *British Buildings*, 1960–4 (1965), 70–9.

Mary de Castro for the predominance in this quarter of the Old Town. The two are to be seen together from many points of view, in odd conjunction. A series of more conventional buildings stretches away to the south, by no means complete as yet. When the plan has been fully developed it opens up the hope of making new and very much more agreeable use of the river front (neglected by Leicester, as by all its neighbours except Bedford and Nottingham).

The site of the Polytechnic is adequate for the moment. But if, in the long run, it should wish or need to grow further, that will not be managed easily. For its territory is strictly finite, bounded on the west by the river, on the north by antiquities (the remains of the Newarke and the Castle), by Oxford Street on the east, and on the south by the Royal Infirmary. The Infirmary is expanding fast too. A new maternity hospital, with 150 beds, was opened here in 1971. Work is proceeding on a Department of Medical Physics, to be followed by a new Out-patients' Department, and then a very large set of buildings in New Bridge Street, providing sixteen operating theatres and 400 surgical beds.[1] This development is long overdue, to meet the growing needs of the region the Infirmary serves. It is now likely to be realised with a speed unlooked-for ten years ago, since the Government's decision in 1970 that the next new Medical School in Britain should be at Leicester. The University hopes to take its first students into the pre-clinical stage in 1975. The students will then proceed to their clinical teaching in and around the Infirmary. The Infirmary too will therefore need, like the Polytechnic, all the space it can get and keep.

If things continue as they are planned at the moment, by the end of the 1970s in the whole of this large area between the Infirmary, the Newarke, and the river there will be scarcely one building that is as much as fifteen years old – unless indeed St Andrew's church in Jarrom Street is spared. One may hope it will be, to serve its original purpose in conditions unimaginably different from those that prevailed when it was built, and to provide a visual counterpoint to all that is being created around it.

Diametrically opposite to this district, on the other side of the Clock Tower, an equally drastic transformation is being carried through in the angle between Belgrave Gate and Humberstone Road. Here the City Council is providing new housing accommodation on a large scale in a variety of dwellings, ranging in height from one storey to more than twenty. The name 'Wharf Street' still survives, but most of its original two-storied houses and shops have gone. On its west side are commercial buildings, including a telephone exchange and the first multi-storey car park that was erected in the centre of Leicester, at Lee Circle. To the north and east lie the new houses and flats, on the St Mark's and St Matthew's Estates. Here is a development of great interest, for it represents the first effort to re-establish

[1] Frizelle and Martin, *Leicester Royal Infirmary*, 219, 224.

housing near the middle of the city. Some of these buildings are only ten minutes' walk from the big stores in Humberstone Gate, from the theatre and other large-scale amusements that are being provided in the Haymarket Centre. Here is part of an answer to the problem of urban decay that confronts Leicester, in common with most other towns of its sort in the Western world. At present, beyond question, the city is almost dead at night, quite dead on Sundays. The whole trend of growth has been outwards, farther and farther into new suburbs and old villages beyond, with the necessary consequence of bringing in more and more private cars, on business or in search of shops and entertainment. Can that trend be reversed? The St Matthew's and St Mark's Estates make the first firm assertion that it can.

The term 're-development' applied to the areas within these Estates is something more than a euphemism for demolition and rebuilding. It connotes far-reaching changes of economic use too. The district comprehended within St Matthew's Estate included, for example, numerous small factories. There were sixty-six of them in 1957, employing on average less than ten people each. By 1970 there were only twenty-seven left, and fifteen of those were on industrial estates: so no more than twelve survived, of the type that characterised the older industrial organisation of Leicester.[1] Before long, we cannot doubt, they will all have disappeared – like blacksmiths' forges, the last of which in the Old Town, off Northgate Street, closed down about 1965.[2] As re-development proceeds, to the north and east of the Clock Tower, all such things will be eliminated. They grew up there haphazardly, as a result of private enterprise – using that phrase in its fullest meaning; they are being removed in consequence of a series of carefully-prepared operations, which are giving whole new quarters to Leicester that have been planned, in their entirety, afresh. There are dangers ahead here, of inflexibility. But then the old 'small-town' firms, and indeed the terraced houses, had their own rigidities too.

It is as yet too early to pronounce any judgment, worth serious attention, on these momentous changes. None of them is yet completed, and the new life and work that they are intended to facilitate needs time for adjustment. Only a very simple view can be offered here of what is being attempted and achieved – so simple that it risks being simple-minded. Materially, it is obvious that a flat on the St Matthew's Estate is incomparably better than a house in Wharf Street. It is new; and it is furnished, to an architect's design, with all the private services that can be reasonably looked for. (It should not be forgotten that, in 1961, more than one in five of the houses in the Leicester district lacked a fixed bath.[3] Every new flat has one.) The public services – transport, schools, day nurseries – are within easy reach; the Estate is to have two doctors' surgeries of its own; there will be a

[1] *Region*, 401.
[2] 41 TLAS (1965–6) 68.
[3] *The East Midlands Study* (1966), 163.

large shopping centre there. A church and a club are to be built. It is here perhaps that one's doubts begin to creep in. When so much is provided, it becomes natural to look for more; but at this point the provision becomes timid, and stops. What are the people who live here going to do with their more and more abundant leisure? They are near enough to the centre of the city to walk in, to enjoy its opportunities and pleasures; and in that they are much more fortunate than, for example, the residents at Rowlatt's Hill or out at Thurnby Lodge. Is this what the majority of them will do? The question will need an answer, based on close observation. It will have an important bearing on the development of the city, well ahead into the twenty-first century.

2

There, then, are some of the ways in which Leicester has been changing physically in recent years. What about the work that goes on in its buildings and streets? That too has changed since the end of the war.

The three leading groups of industries remain – hosiery, footwear, and engineering; they have not been joined by a fourth. But in terms of the employment they offer, their relative importance has altered. The footwear industry now stands decidedly behind the other two. It has been going through difficulties in Leicester, where for a very long time past it has concentrated chiefly on shoes for women and children. In this branch of the business – though not in the manufacture of men's footwear – Britain has lost ground, particularly to Italy. The plastic materials that have become increasingly popular at the expense of leather can be used economically only in mass production; and that has placed many of the smaller manufacturers, characteristic of Leicester, at a disadvantage. The trend in most industries everywhere in the country, towards the absorption of small firms into large combines, has been very evident in the Leicester shoe manufacture. One or two large family firms remain. The oldest of them now is Portland Shoes Ltd, founded more than a century ago. Stead & Simpson's, who played a notable part in the introduction of the industry into Leicester, are also still independent, with their chain of 250 retail shops throughout the country. But important and respected as these firms are, they are entirely overshadowed in size by the British Shoe Corporation Footwear Group.[1] That Group has now absorbed, directly or indirectly, most of the other well-known Leicester firms in the business, headed by Freeman Hardy & Willis.

The manufacture of hosiery and other textiles continues to play a great part in the economy of Leicester. Here too the number of people employed has, on the

[1] *Region*, 381–2, 411–12.

face of it, declined; but that is in part due to a re-location of the industry, many new factories having been opened just outside the city boundaries, particularly in Wigston.

The textile manufacture today employs about the same number of people in Leicester as engineering, the third main group of its industries. The city retains its supremacy in the making of the machines required in the hosiery and footwear manufactures: the British United Company turns out more than four-fifths of the shoe-making machinery in the country.[1] Most of the familiar, old-established Leicester firms – including all those mentioned in the early history of the industry on pp. 2–3 – are still in business, though many have now become part of national or international combines. Cort's is now Sankey Corts Ltd; Imperial Typewriters passed into association with the American Litton Industries in 1966;[2] Goodwin Barsby was taken over by the Aveling-Barford Group in 1954 and then, after thirteen years, passed with that Group into the Leyland Motor Corporation, and so into British Leyland.[3]

Nevertheless, it would be wrong to imply that the city's current economic development comprises nothing but the continuance and extension of its old-established industries. Some new enterprises have appeared, and they are occasionally startling. Leicester is almost the last place in which one would expect to find the chief European manufacturer of sailing dinghies; but the Bell Woodworking Co. Ltd could claim that position.[4] There are not many other striking newcomers, however, and two reasons can be put forward for that. The high rate of employment consistently maintained by the city naturally discourages new firms looking for labour; and, on the same account, the Government has deliberately hampered or prevented the establishment of new industries here, doing all it can to divert them to those parts of the country in which there is serious unemployment.

So, although there has been much change of emphasis, and even more in techniques, the ground-pattern of Leicester's industries continues to resemble very closely the pattern established in 1939 – one might almost say in 1914. Nearly all the old features persist: the predominance of the same three industries, the high rate of employment, the equally heavy demand for the labour of women and men. But there is one most significant difference: the steady diminution in the number and power of the family firms. They are still to be found, in all the city's chief industries. Two of those in the shoe trade have been mentioned already. In hosiery we might take, as one example out of many, Pick & Sons Ltd;[5] in engineering

[1] *Ibid.*, 383.
[2] *Ibid.*, 419.
[3] R. E. Pochin, *Over my Shoulder and Beyond* (1971), 92, 107.
[4] *Region*, 423.
[5] For its history cf. J. B. Pick, *The Pick Knitwear Story*, 1856–1956.

Gimson's – a firm that can justly claim a certain historical primacy among its fellows. It will be many years before all such businesses vanish. When the last of them closes or is taken over, it will be time to say that the old Leicester has gone.

The implications of this change reach deep and far. It is just 300 years now since the modern industrial development of Leicester began, with the introduction of the stocking-frame; and the whole course of that development, until our own time, has been moulded by the enterprise of the family business. We can trace it in the Freemen's Register, with minute exactitude, in the eighteenth century; in the nineteenth, it is written all over the history of the town, not in its commercial affairs alone but also in its political and social life. For, with surprisingly few exceptions, in almost any field that can be named (other than the strictly professional) the leadership came from the industrialists, the men who had made these firms or inherited their place in them. And, as we have seen, the firms were small. No triton swam among these minnows.

In the past, under the old conditions, the life of the town – in religion and charity and politics, no less than industry and trade – was dominated by a quite small group of families, most of whom were related to one another. At times they very obviously formed cliques, even one or two governing cliques, as in the 1830s and 1840s; and that sometimes occasioned a natural resentment. More usually, however, their ascendancy was exercised with the mildest restraint, in a way that could hardly offend anybody – very often indeed to the evident advantage of the town, which profited from these people's unobtrusive benevolence.[1]

The supremacy was broken after 1918, when organised labour began to play its full part in politics. Its leaders were of a different social class and were, in the nature of the case, antagonistic to any such predominance. But, except in strictly political terms, there was little conflict here. Great good sense prevailed, and there was room for a time for the older and the newer modes of thought and action to work side by side. To some extent, even, they became fused. This was an important force in keeping down conflict in the city during the years between the Wars. Now however – as a result not of conflict, but of economic changes that have swept through the whole Western world – that equilibrium has been destroyed. Only a small part of Leicester's industry can be said to be controlled within Leicester today. The economic destiny of the city is determined more and more by boards of directors meeting in London or across the Atlantic, and locally by those who are essentially managers, responsible to them.

Nor is this true of industry alone. Exactly the same change has taken place in retail trade. Here a revolution – that term seems justified – has been carried

---

[1] It is reflected, un-selfconsciously and in its most attractive form, in Mrs Ellis's *Records of Nineteenth Century Leicester*.

through in the course of a very short time. In fact, it can be dated quite precisely. It began with the opening of the first supermarkets on the American model, in the middle of the city, about 1960, in and near the Market Place. It was completed on 6 February 1971, when Messrs Simpkin & James, provision merchants, closed down. Their premises ran through from the Market Place to Horsefair Street which made access and parking difficult. In the course of those years, many other corresponding changes had occurred: the opening of new supermarkets galore, including the translation of Messrs Sainsbury's in 1963 from its poky and inconvenient pair of shops on the corner of Cank Street and Cheapside to purpose-built premises a quarter of a mile down Humberstone Gate; the appearance of the Woolco store at Oadby (cf. p. 130); the closing of almost all the major locally-owned shops in the centre of the city, like Morley's drapery and the ironmonger's business of Messrs Pochin in Granby Street; the purchase of Joseph Johnson's store by Fenwick's of Newcastle in 1963.

No single event in this series made so much impression in Leicester as the closing of Simpkin & James. It was mourned by countless people who never dealt there but regarded it as a symbol of an older and still cherished world; by others who used it constantly and grumbled at its cramped premises and slow service; by very many more who, though they also grumbled on occasion, saw it as the one shop of its kind that was left in which standards of high quality were still anxiously maintained, where service was still personal and usually obliging. These constant and loyal customers were not all by any means rich. Whenever one had leisure, or room, to pause in Simpkin's and look around, one was certain to be struck by the miscellany of social class that one saw there. The customers had one thing in common: they wanted good provisions, and they relied on the old-fashioned firm to supply them. For most things they paid a penny or a shilling more there than they would at a supermarket – though not for all: to the very end the shop purveyed bacon that was not only better than its rivals' but, cut for cut, frequently cheaper. And when it came to the best things – to Suffolk hams or Carlsbad plums at Christmas, to cheese from all over England and Europe, cut freshly for the customer and not pre-packed, to flowers to be sent to a hospital – there was nothing to touch Simpkin's. It was rare, too, among shops of its kind in the provinces in having a really well-stocked wine department, with cellars stretching under the Market Place. And finally it had a café upstairs, a little cramped and inconvenient like the shop itself, but furnished in every article in the style of the 1930s, where one was waited on with the old politeness to the end.

The closing of Simpkin & James was the subject of an ITV programme, put out on 13 April following. It was not generally thought to be good, either by local people or by the professional critics of the London papers. The *Leicester Mercury* remarked that it was 'an embarrassing reflection [of the city] seen, as it were,

17a. The University: Engineering Building (Stirling & Gowan, 1963).

17b. City of Leicester College of Education, Scraptoft (Bridgwater & Shepheard, 1960). The old Hall (Plate 22b) appears in the bottom right-hand corner.

18a. Auditorium of the Theatre Royal (p. 39). Architect William Parsons. Demolished 1958.

18b. Haymarket Theatre (City Architect, Stephen George, 1973).

19a. St Matthew's Estate (cf. pp. 91–2). Looking E. from the junction of Ottawa Road and Christow Street. City Architect, Stephen George.

19b. The Holiday Inn (1971). Architect William Bond of Memphis, Tennessee.

20. The rebuilding of the city in the late 1960s. The broad roadway is Charles Street (p. 69), joining Belgrave Gate. On its left side are the back premises of the Bell (p. 53); on the right Epic House, and to the right of that Lee Circle car park. This was the first multi-storey car park in Leicester; a second (that now surmounted by the Abbey Motor Hotel) is under construction in the centre of the picture. In the top right-hand corner St Mark's church; along the top of the picture the canal, and beyond it the Abbey Park.

21a. Wigston Magna: 42-4 Bushloe End, with its hosiery workshop at the rear.

21b. Interior of the workshop, with stocking frames. Photographs taken 1972.

22a. Oadby: Middlemeade, Stoughton Drive South (architect, Stockdale Harrison). Now part of Beaumont Hall, University of Leicester.

22b. Scraptoft Hall (date on rainwater head 1723). Now part of City of Leicester College of Education (cf. Plate 17b).

23a. Wigston Magna: alabaster font in All Saints church.

23b. Evington church: W. window of N. aisle, early fourteenth century. Drawing by J. C. Buckler (BM Add. MS. 36979, fol. 42).

24. Two County Council buildings: (a) County Rooms, Hotel Street (John Johnson, 1800; i. 140–1), with the windows restored to their original form in 1973. (b) County Hall, Glenfield (County Architect, T. A. Collins, 1969).

through a distorting mirror'.[1] But the interesting thing is that the programme was made at all. It showed at any rate an awareness that the event was historic, and not alone for the community of Leicester.

These trends are all in the same direction, and it would be foolish to deplore them. The old society, so deeply rooted here, had many faults: above all, perhaps, those that come from narrow vision and a limited experience of the world. A great deal of fresh life has been brought into the city by those whom we may perhaps call, in the phrase of a Leicester author, the New Men. The most generous gifts that have been made to it in recent years have come, for example, from Sir Charles Keene, who has served it devotedly as a Labour politician; from Dr Mac Goldsmith, an industrialist who was born neither in Leicester nor in Britain. The city has made some admired contributions towards solving the intractable problems of traffic control and town planning in our time. They are due primarily to Mr W. K. Smigielski, who was its Planning Officer from 1962 to 1972. He was born in Poland, and came to Leicester from Leeds.

Or we can see this development in another way. The small University College, whose early history we have traced, started to expand in the years immediately following the end of the Second World War. In 1945–6 it had 109 full-time students. When, in 1957, it became an independent University, it had 816. The number is now approaching 4,000.[2] It is unrecognisably different from what it was in its early days, not merely because it is so vastly bigger. Equally important, it is an institution of a kind totally unlike what its founders envisaged. They thought of it entirely in local terms; and their thoughts were in harmony with those that prevailed everywhere in England at that time. The College was to draw its students predominantly from the city and its immediate neighbourhood; and so it did until 1946.[3] Then, when its expansion began, its students came from all over England and Wales, and a fair number from overseas. This arose not from any deliberate action on the College's part but from a change in the Government's policy in making grants to students, allowing them to go to any university or college that would admit them.[4]

At the same time the expansion of the academic and administrative staff brought into Leicester an increasing number of people, highly skilled in their own lines, who settled in the city as strangers. Its first and second Vice-Chancellors, Sir

[1] LM 14 April 1971. For other comments cf. *Daily Telegraph*, 14 April, and *Observer*, 18 April.

[2] The growth of the University in these years is recorded in Simmons, *New University*, chaps. vii and viii, and by Prof. A. J. Allaway in *Region*, 537–50.

[3] Of the 159 students (full-time and part-time) at the College in 1938–9, 132 came from Leicester, Leicestershire, and the adjoining counties: *Annual Report*, 1938–9, 15–16.

[4] On this point see Simmons, *New University*, 140–1.

E

Charles Wilson and Sir Fraser Noble, have both been elected to the office of the highest academic responsibility in Britain, the Chairmanship of the Committee of Vice-Chancellors and Principals. The succession of formal heads of the institution was symbolic. The last President of the College was the 9th Duke of Rutland, one of the great territorial magnates of England; the first Chancellor Lord Adrian, O.M., who was among the most distinguished men of science of his age.

It is often said, nevertheless, that the University does little for Leicester, that it exists in isolation from the city in which it is placed. That is true, and false. It now educates few students from Leicester schools. It grows according to its own academic needs, not according to the demands that may be put forward by the community. Even its buildings have been, with some exceptions, designed by architects from outside Leicester; only a few of them have been built by local contractors. (This has not been a matter of policy; it has resulted from the increasing complexity and specialisation in this kind of building, and the practices that have to be followed in dealing with the University Grants Committee, which is the paymaster.) It is understandable that the citizen of Leicester, driving along University Road, should feel that this range of large buildings has nothing whatever to say to him, that the University has come to be sited in the city by some kind of accident. By contrast he thinks perhaps of the Polytechnic, which is more intimately a part of Leicester itself: a child of the Corporation, whose work has been devoted in the past almost wholly to studies appropriate to the place, of evident practical value.

But that contrast is much too simple. As the Polytechnic grows, its studies reach out far beyond the immediately useful, into fields of research just as remote from the interest of that citizen as the University's. And although it is situated nearer the centre of Leicester, not raised superciliously above it, the Polytechnic's site is fast becoming hardly less of an enclave of its own.

Universities must always, in large measure, look inwards, their work proceeding independently of their surroundings; their members tend naturally to communicate with their fellows in other universities, who are engaged in the same pursuits. The demand that they should 'serve their community', as if they were schools, is therefore misdirected. Much of what they do is of no interest to that community at all. It may be that the modern British vogue for placing universities well away from the centres of towns or right outside them (a vogue in which the College at Leicester was unintentionally a pioneer) has accentuated this separation, by comparison say with Cambridge or Utrecht or Salamanca, where the university and the town are one; but the separation will always be there. It need not be absolute. Certainly it is not so at Leicester, where the University and the Polytechnic both offer a great deal to the city: free lunch-time concerts, lectures, drama, vigorous adult education. Their students have contributed generously, and sometimes with imagination, to the social work of the city. Leicester owes the Phoenix Theatre, and its civic successor, very largely to a partnership between the two Professors of English in the University and two or three Leicester business men, collaborating with sympathisers on the City Council.

If the University has grown into something unrecognisably different from what its first sponsors envisaged, that is the way of all human creations that develop a life of their own. Though it may appear aloof on its hill, it does in fact do a good deal in and for the city to which it owes its foundation; and as its Medical School develops in the later 1970s it will be seen to do much more.

3

In the first week of 1970 the *Leicester Mercury* published a review of the previous decade and a forecast for the one that was opening, written by a shrewd and experienced observer, Mr William Kidd.[1] His account of the sixties was almost uniformly sombre. He saw the city afflicted with Planning Blight, which he argued was even more dangerous to its good health than the difficulties of handling traffic and the racial problems arising out of immigration from overseas. The City Planning Department instituted in 1962 had produced its Traffic Plan in 1964: vigorous, original at some points, enterprising – and, as he pointed out, still a dead letter six years afterwards. The expenditure it called for had been refused owing to the economic troubles of the years following its production. And then, in 1967, came the beginning of the inquiry into the reorganisation of local government, inducing in this as in so many other matters a disposition to stand still, waiting to see what was to happen.

In the same years plans had been accepted for the erection of a very large new Civic Centre, occupying the whole territory between the New Walk and the London Road station. The case for it was essentially the same as the case for a new Town Hall in the Victorian age. The municipal administration was growing fast, and its officers were scattered around inefficiently, when they needed to be united for easy and continuous consultation. Just as in 1840–70, there was protracted argument, to some extent along much the same lines. But the outcome was different: for this time the scheme was first knocked on the head by its cost and then killed by the review of local government, decreed in London. Meanwhile a large tract of central land had been closed to all other development: it had simply stood empty, used as a car park.

Nor was this all. A long and bitter argument had been in progress since 1961

[1] LM 2, 9, 16 January 1970.

about the re-development of the Market Place. The City Planning Officer, Mr Smigielski, had put forward an imaginative scheme for it, whose progress had ground to a halt in the face of embattled uncomprehending resistance. The rebuilding of almost the whole of the big triangular site between Belgrave Gate, Charles Street, and Humberstone Gate had been decided on, but not implemented. The East Midlands Region was much worse provided with hotel accommodation than any other in the whole country;[1] and Leicester was a black spot even in that region. Repeated attempts had been made to build a major hotel in the city. All had failed. As Mr Kidd's recital went on, it grew into a reasoned indictment of 'the unkept promises, the shabby image of the past decade'.

And yet, within two years, things came to look different. The reconstruction of the Market Place was completed in 1971: not indeed in the ideal form Mr Smigielski had first conceived, but still in a way that greatly improved the comfort of buying and selling there, and at the same time added a new visual amenity to Leicester. For now a little square was opened in front of the Corn Exchange, enabling Ordish's noble staircase to be seen, letting air and light into the middle of the market itself. This was a thoroughly successful operation: the memorial at once of a sensitive eye and of a perseverance not to be discouraged.

The big Haymarket Centre has, in fact been built. The shopping centre was formally opened on 5 June 1973; the theatre on 17 October following. We have yet to see how it will turn out, but at least the scheme is being realised. And the new hotel, the Holiday Inn – the first large hotel to be built in the city since 1898 – was opened in 1971.[2] So some of the promises of the 'sixties are at length being redeemed.

These things are satisfactory. The progress report was much better, by the end of 1971, than Mr Kidd had thought possible at the beginning of 1970. The reconstruction of part of Belgrave Gate – the motorist's chief plague spot in Leicester – is under way, together with much more new Council housing in that quarter. Some of the Planning Blight has been removed through the release of a part of the land previously held for future development near the railway station, and building proceeds actively there now.

In December 1970 the restrictions on office building imposed by the Government in 1966 were removed. They had borne particularly heavily on Leicester. Whereas in 1966–9 seven applications out of eight for licences to erect office

[1] *Britain and International Tourism* (HMSO, 1972), 30.
[2] Given its situation and architecture, the name of this establishment could scarcely be more absurd: for who wants to spend his holiday on a roundabout, or associates the cosiness of an 'inn' with nine stories of concrete? But the name is no more than a comic accident: the name borne by all the hotels, irrespective of situation, in the vast American chain to which this one belongs.

buildings in Nottingham and Derby had been successful, in Leicester two out of three had been rejected.[1] Leicester had been paying the price of its relative comfort and affluence. Now, in this respect, the brake was taken off, with consequences potentially important for the planning of the future.

Many of Mr Kidd's strictures still remain valid, nevertheless. The brave Traffic Plan of 1964 has not been implemented. Mr Smigielski's repeated demands that the motor car should be banned throughout the centre of the city, echoed by planners in other cities up and down the country, are not being met – apart from a timid beginning in Gallowtree Gate. Mr Kidd's fears for the industrial development of the city must continue to be disquieting. If that development is to be thwarted by the Government in the interests of towns or regions where there is more unemployment, then may Leicester itself not become, for industry and all those who work in it, a seedy and mediocre place by the 1980s?

4

Leicester is suffering, then, from many troubles inherited from the past and from some that are the product of our own time. In the 'sixties, though its traditional prosperity continued, it bore some of the signs of anxiety, and beyond question it earned the epithet its critics sometimes applied to it, a 'shabby city'.

The phrase was frequently used by Mr Smigielski, in token not of contempt but of disappointed affection;[2] and he strove valiantly to take away the reproach. It was a steady battle, here as everywhere else in Britain, against the litter louts, against the mere wastefulness of the commercial and social habits of our time. If the battle could not be entirely won, some notable successes were achieved. Town Hall Square was tidied up and slightly remodelled, to become on summer days once more a pleasant place to sit and rest in, under the shadow of the Town Hall itself, rejuvenated by cleaning, sparkling as when it was new. The re-thinking of the shape of the city's roads made it possible to reprieve the Crescent, which was then refurbished by private enterprise, to take a leading place once again among the distinguished buildings of Leicester. But the chief battle has been fought in New Walk.

The New Walk has long been recognised as Leicester's special distinction. Nothing like it is to be found anywhere else in Britain. It can only remind us of the shady boulevards laid out on the site of fortifications, say in Senlis or some other

[1] *Office Services in the East Midlands* (East Midlands Economic Planning Council, ?1971), vi, 258.
[2] Cf. the article, with its telling pictures, in *Leicester Chronicle*, 3 November 1967.

fortunate town in France. It was planned and planted as a promenade and always used as such – an extended 'pedestrian precinct', like those which modern towns are striving at great cost to create. Wheeled traffic has at all times been excluded from its whole length. Two squares open out of it, and a railed-in 'oval' towards the top. The Walk became lined with houses only very gradually, between about 1825 and 1895.[1] It remained in residential occupation until after the first War, when some of its houses began to become offices and hotels. The lower end then slowly deteriorated. By 1950 the whole had come to make a very odd mixture. There were tatty little offices at the foot. Then came Holy Cross Priory, faced by terraces of houses, some of which were well kept as offices and others decaying fast as dwellings. The worst group of houses was immediately above the Priory, and they formed a sad little slum. There was nothing so squalid again higher up; but the use, and the maintenance, of the property varied startlingly. The tall Late-Victorian houses at the top, in Upper New Walk, were then passing out of private occupation.

Mr Kidd's Blight was seen here at its most discreditable all through the 'fifties and 'sixties. Leicester's special distinction had become its special shame. No one appeared able or willing to take any action at all, until at length in 1967 Mr Smigielski's Planning Department came forward with a set of considered proposals for the rehabilitation of the New Walk from top to bottom. They involved a minimum of demolition. The peculiarly dilapidated group of houses had to go. They were undistinguished, and no serious loss in themselves. In its original form the plan proposed the reconstruction of the largest terrace, on the west side, behind its old façade. What appeared was a wholly new building, a rather unhappy blend of the early nineteenth century and the late twentieth, with a frankly twentieth-century block opposite. For the rest it was refurbishing, no more, and it was intelligently done. The front of the Museum was cleared, with excellent effect (vol i, Plate 24), the squares tidied up. Everywhere it became plain that the Walk was cared for at last. One has only to stroll along it at lunch time on a bright spring or autumn day to see how much it is appreciated now.

It may not be widely realised just how deep was the disgust that the squalor of New Walk had inspired. A few years ago, when the plan for improving it had been published but not carried into effect, I happened to meet there an old friend, a distinguished native of Leicester. He no longer lives in the city, but he revisits it occasionally, and he remarked to me, with an intensity of bitterness that is not characteristic of him, on the filthiness and philistinism of the whole place. When I told him what was now intended, he was incredulous, making it clear that he did not suppose for one minute that the work would ever be carried into effect. If

[1] See C. Potts in 44 TLAS (1968–9) 76–85 and in Growth of Leicester, ed. Brown, 56–61.

he now sees the result, he will perhaps recognise that there is a genuine spirit of improvement at work in his native city, battling continually against the forces of drab ignorant commercialism that he despises and rightly detests.

There have been welcome signs, then, that the civic authority is aware that Leicester presents at many points a seedy appearance and that that discredit ought to be removed. It may be added that the County Council has shown itself commendably solicitous for the historic buildings it owns in the city. It has carried through a delightful renovation of Castle House, to serve as the Judges' Lodgings in place of John Johnson's County Rooms – which were not designed for that purpose, and never fulfilled it well. Now that the Council has removed all its work out to Glenfield (see p. 134), the Rooms are no longer needed for administrative business. They have been cleaned and restored, if not with unfailing taste yet with affection. The plate-glass windows that have been a blot on the building for over 100 years have been replaced by others following the original design (how many other local authorities in the country would be prepared to incur expenditure in such a way as that?), and the Rooms are now coming to take a part in the social life of the city something like that which they served when they were new, in the opening years of the nineteenth century (Plate 24a).

All this concerns the centre of the city, where the chief monuments of the past are concentrated. But some attention is also being given to the suburbs. The Housing Act of 1969 put forward the conception of General Improvement Areas. The Leicester Housing Committee responded quickly, in February 1971, with a pioneer plan for Clarendon Park.[1] Its first objective was, rightly, the improvement of houses. Though Clarendon Park is a development of the very late nineteenth century, when the main lessons of sanitation had come to be fully accepted, and though it was given a water supply of its own (see p. 12), in 1971 over 45 per cent of the houses in the district still lacked either a bathroom, main water, or an inside lavatory. Liberal grants were now offered to the owners of these houses for supplying their defects and carrying out repairs where they were needed. At the same time the Housing Committee put forward proposals for improving the flow of traffic through the whole group of streets in the area, for creating small paved open spaces, and for extending the provision of trees. The plan itself is simply and cogently presented. Any one who is familiar with the area and studies these proposals must be impressed by them, by the care, imagination, and economy they show. Here is a chance to intervene, at just the right moment and in the right way, to prevent the deterioration of ageing property, to adapt it to changing conditions, and so to give it a long new lease of life. It is much to be hoped that the residents

[1] *Clarendon Park General Improvement Area* (City of Leicester Housing Committee, 1971).

and the owners of the houses concerned will appreciate the opportunity that is being offered to them, and respond to it.[1]

This is the first such scheme to be brought forward. It is to be followed by others, notably by one for the much larger Highfields, the district in the city that gives ground for the gravest concern. It began life, as we have seen (p. 10), 100 years ago as a prosperous suburb; but with the steady migration of the middle classes, to the outer fringes of the enlarged town and then to the country, its condition slowly deteriorated. Its ample houses were cut up, first into flats and then into units of one room. By the 1950s it had come to offer exactly the kind of quarters that poor people with large families would be looking for on their arrival in the city. And it was people just of this sort who began to come to Leicester in large numbers at this time.

The city had not attracted immigrants from overseas on any substantial scale before. It did so now chiefly because it offered abundant work of certain types to which they were suited. At first the greatest number came from the West Indies, where over-population and under-employment were particularly pressing; then followed a steady and larger flow from India, with some from Pakistan. In the late 'sixties there came a change. In 1966 it was reckoned that West Indians comprised a quarter of the whole immigrant population. Five years later that figure had been halved; similarly the Indian and Pakistani population had been reduced from over 50 per cent to 40 per cent. In replacement there had appeared an influx from Kenya – to make up nearly 40 per cent of the total; and of this group more than three-quarters were Asians. By 1971 Leicester had the highest concentration of East African Asians anywhere in Britain.[2] Already in 1968 it was thought that immigrants from overseas comprised a tenth of the whole population of the city; three years later they were supposed to number some 36,000. Their children certainly formed 17 per cent of the city's school population.[3] Then in the summer of 1972, suddenly, came the expulsion of Asians from Uganda. Although they were discouraged, before leaving their own country, from making for Leicester, large numbers came there nevertheless. In May 1973 it was estimated that nearly 4,500 had 'established a settled abode' in the city.[4]

The notes of caution here in stating figures are highly necessary. From the outset one of the difficulties that this immigration had presented was that so much

---

[1] The plan has met with sharp criticism from some of the residents: see *Leicester Chronicle*, 6 October 1972.

[2] *The Times*, 4 November 1972.

[3] RMOH 1971, 54. On the other hand the census of 1971 showed no more than 23,280 people from the countries of the 'New Commonwealth': 8.2 per cent of the whole population of the city.

[4] RMOH 1972, 52–3.

of it was transient. The newly-arrived people settled where they could find shelter; they tended to move frequently, within Leicester and to and from other towns. It was impossible for any officials to keep track of them.[1] The Medical Officer of Health put the matter quite clearly in 1972: 'We do not even know accurately the total number of immigrants in Leicester, let alone the size and structure of their families'.[2]

There could be no doubt, however, in broad terms about some of the problems that this influx posed. It was a matter of housing – that first of all; and it was disquieting, however natural, that so large a proportion of the arrivals should have gone to the Highfields. In cities where there had been communities of this kind established much longer – in Bradford, for example – whole quarters had come to be occupied by them, with the most evidently undesirable social consequences.

In the long run it may well appear that the greatest difficulties arose in education and in public health. Many sorts of expedients had to be adopted in order to teach the children: the provision of mobile class-rooms, the opening of new schools for them in reconditioned buildings (as at Duxbury Road in 1968), the conveyance of children by bus, sometimes over substantial distances, to less crowded schools in outer districts.[3] But accommodation presented only one of the educational problems – the most urgent, perhaps, but in some senses the simplest. The teaching of the children, given difficulties of language and social custom, was a greater one. It was hard not only to communicate effectively but also to assess the children's capabilities. Nor was it only children who had to be provided for; it was almost as necessary to help those beyond the school age to adjust themselves to their life in Britain. In 1971 a new institution was set up to provide courses for immigrants aged sixteen and upwards, as an annexe to the South Fields College of Further Education.[4]

The health service was tested severely. Again the difficulties arose largely from language, and they stretched the doctors and the staff in all departments, for it naturally took on average longer to deal with each individual case among these people.[5] In one respect the arrival of the immigrants produced a marked change in the general pattern of the city's health. In the 1950s it had seemed that tuberculosis was a disease so greatly on the wane that it might disappear. It now returned, the immigrants from India and Pakistan being particularly susceptible to it. By

[1] Cf. *ibid.*, 1962, viii; 1968, 7.
[2] *ibid.*, 1972, 52.
[3] Education Committee, *Report*, 1967, 11; 1968,
[4] *Ibid.*, 1971, 8.
[5] RMOH 1971, 55.

1967 the number of cases of the disease among Asians came to exceed those among the white population in the city.[1]

The relationship between the immigrants and their neighbours gave rise to many further difficulties – and again they arose from misunderstanding more than from any other cause. The usual hostilities appeared: notices in windows, for example, 'No coloureds. Go away'. There were occasional assaults on the newcomers and the houses they were living in. One of these disturbances threatened to spill over into trouble involving the police in 1965. The inquiry that followed revealed that though the animosity was certainly there the matters complained of arose almost entirely from the inability of the immigrants and the police to communicate.[2] Given this explosive situation, however, what strikes one most is the small number of outbreaks of disorder. No one could pretend that these immigrants were welcomed with any warmth. Yet many of them settled in Leicester and gave clear signs that they had come to regard it, for all its imperfections, as their home.

5

A sensible citizen of Leicester, in the 1960s and 1970s, could not possibly feel that all was well with it. He might be forgiven for thinking that, judged by almost any test, the true values and pleasures of life, here as elsewhere, were being constantly debased; and his view of the future of the city might well be gloomy almost to despair. Such feelings are not without their precedent. A good many of the towns-people must have thought much the same, in their hearts, in the 1540s, at the onset of the Reformation; and about 1oo years after that, in the shocking turmoil of the Civil War. We should probably be right in saying that a majority of the hosiery workers felt an even greater despondency, beyond any hope of cure, in the 1830s and 1840s. It is worth remembering such things, for each seemed disastrous at the time and yet sooner or later there was a recovery and the society righted itself, sometimes in strange ways, unpredictable. No prophecy is offered here; nothing more than an attempt to record something of the mood of the time, to express its uncertainties and fears, its disillusion – while also recalling the consolations that can be derived from a hard-headed study of the past. And even if the generally desponding view put forward here is accepted – as, by many people, it will not be – it should be tempered not only by notions derived from the past, but also in some degree by a number of things that have happened lately, in Mr Kidd's deplorable 'sixties. One or two instances concerning the physical environment have just been mentioned. There are more, of other kinds.

[1] *Ibid.*, 1963, 55; 1964, 53; 1967, 71; 1968, 7.
[2] *The Times*, 4 March, 5 April 1965; LM 6 April 1965.

We have noted how seldom in the past the city has shown itself an innovator. It may well have done wisely to wait, as so often, to see the effect of a new policy or practice, adopting it only when it has shown its worth, and then perhaps in a form improved by experience. That was the way it acted over most public utilities in the nineteenth century, and it would be hard to demonstrate that, on balance, the citizens lost much in consequence. But caution, though it may be sensible, is totally uninspiring; and inspiration has indeed been offered very rarely in Leicester. During the 1960s, in a number of small ways, there were some signs that this stance was being changed.

In Robert Mark, for instance, the city had an outstanding Chief Constable, who was not only efficient but reflective and outspoken. He was willing to make himself responsible for recommending experiment. Under his guidance Leicester was one of the pioneers in establishing traffic wardens, in 1961. Reviewing the results of this policy two years later, he felt able to claim not only that it had eased the control of parking in the city but that the wardens had freed the police to undertake the specially important duties that belonged to them alone. The number of arrests made at or near the scene of a crime had doubled in the course of those two years.[1] The system that worked, on the whole, so smoothly in Leicester came to be adopted widely in other towns in Britain.

Mr Mark was anxious to extend the use of traffic wardens by employing them on point duty – so, again, releasing constables for other tasks. Here, however, he was moving too fast. The proposal was turned down by the Home Office. Since then its decision has been rescinded. So that every time he sees today a traffic warden directing traffic, say at Oxford Circus, a Leicester man is entitled to feel that his city has set an example to London.

Again – and in the light of past experience, what change could be more surprising? – the theatre now became an effective force in the city. The 1950s had closed with the demolition of the Palace, the last professional theatre left. The only drama then presented came from the amateurs of the Little Theatre, an enterprise founded in 1922, which battled on undaunted and had even been brave enough to reconstruct its building when that was burnt down in 1955. The Corporation was now persuaded to extend its patronage to the drama, as it had not done since the reign of Charles I. It agreed to accept the cost of erecting a new small theatre as a temporary measure, to be succeeded by a larger permanent one at a later date The Phoenix, opened in 1963, was the result: a tiny theatre indeed, offering only some 270 seats, and built for the remarkably small sum of £30,000. Commendably cheap, it proved far from nasty, establishing itself with particular warmth in the liking of those who acted there.[2] The Corporation's other promise has now been

[1] R. Mark, *A Police View of the Control of Parking in Urban Areas* (1963), 15.
[2] Cf. *Region*, 568.

fulfilled with a theatre to hold about three times as many people at the Haymarket Centre. It would be wrong to say that Leicester has at last achieved its theatrical salvation. Even in the small theatre there were times when the attendance was disquietingly thin, and it has yet to be seen how steadily the new one can be filled. But the theatre is certainly very much better established in Leicester – offering a wide range of plays, old and new and mostly good – than it has been at any time in the past.

In the 'sixties also Leicester acquired its own radio station; and here it is entitled to make a modest claim as a pioneer. When the BBC decided to establish a network of local broadcasting, in terms of the White Paper *Broadcasting Policy* of 1966, it negotiated agreements with a number of local authorities. One was the Corporation of Leicester, whose response was prompt, straightforward, and liberal. It agreed to underwrite the cost of running the station for an experimental period of two years. Of the other seven stations established in this first phase, only that of Stoke-on-Trent was supported so completely by its civic authority. Radio Leicester was the first of all these stations to open, on 8 November 1967.

The City Council was much criticised for the expenditure it incurred in this way: by those who saw other uses for the £60,000 it had thus agreed to spend, over the two years; by those who saw no value in the idea, as well as by those who were well aware of its value and wished to have a hand in establishing a commercial station themselves; by those who argued that, since its programmes could be made available only on VHF, it would not be able to reach an audience large enough to justify the venture. The agreement was maintained, however, fairly and honourably, without question.

It is not easy to appraise the station's success.[1] The small staff that served it worked very hard, to produce four or five hours' broadcasting of their own (apart from what they relayed from the BBC networks) each day; and some of the regular programmes established themselves as intelligent commentary or good entertainment, or as both. But even if the number of those listening to Radio Leicester could be precisely established, we should still not know what impact it made: just as a newspaper's figures of circulation are no guide to the effect it has on the minds of its readers. One thing, however, can be said – and this weighed with a good many members of the City Council when the matter was debated: that since 1963, when the *Evening Mail* was discontinued, Leicester had been reduced to a single daily paper, the *Mercury*. It seemed to many people a good thing in itself that the purveyance of local news should not be a monopoly. Competition in presenting it, in a different medium appealing in a different way, could hardly be anything but beneficial. To people who thought in this fashion, the radio complemented the

[1] A report on the first year of its operation was published: *Radio Leicester: the First Year* [1968].

newspaper. Taken together, they could hope to offer a more effective and complete presentation of the activities, the interests and hopes of the community than either of them could achieve alone. The technical limitation to VHF was indeed a serious drawback to the station; but that was removed in 1972, when it began to broadcast on the medium waveband.

What has just been said need imply no criticism of the *Mercury*. Indeed, towards the conclusion of a study that has been largely concerned with the last two centuries, it would be ungracious to express anything but gratitude to it, and to all the newspapers that have served Leicester in succession. They enjoy one advantage that neither radio nor television can ever command: all their words are permanently recorded, in print. In common with other newspapers at all times, the *Mercury* has chosen to express its own opinions and to present its news in accordance with them. The critical reader, whether on the day the paper is published or twenty years or a century afterwards, will always look for the influence of those opinions, and allow for them in what he reads. He will find them at times disconcertingly volatile – as, for instance, on the issue of the preservation of Town Hall Square; but then he will recognise that that volatility has its own explanation, and he will be stimulated to search for it. Almost all the most powerful forces in our world make against the calm judicious presentation of news, and the considered commentary on it; to many people now, the London press presents a most unpleasing spectacle. If they look closely at the *Leicester Mercury* in the 1960s they may find it, like its London counterparts, less informative than its predecessors of the 1860s, heavily dominated as it has to be by advertisement. They may find some of the opinions expressed there curious or shocking. But at least they will recognise that the city still had an organ of news and comment that did declare an opinion and that did – with whatever faults and omissions – record the news of Leicester day by day; and for those things they must always be grateful to it.

6

So we can see much that is disturbing in the recent history of Leicester, and at least a little that gives cause for congratulation and hope. One other thing remains to be noted: something not positive but negative, which yet is important and shows that Leicester still remains true to the character it has borne in the past. In our violent times, it has remained up to now a comparatively peaceful place.

There have been many bitter arguments in the city during these years on political and social questions: on comprehensive schools, for example, on alien immigration, on housing, on the development of industry. In the twentieth century – unlike the nineteenth – the battle of parties in the Council has been real, and even. The balance has swayed this way and that. In 1953 there was a Labour majority of fourteen; in 1969 a Conservative majority of forty-four. But the victors have not made the mistake of trampling on the vanquished. They have seen, to put it no higher, that it may be their turn next. So it has been the usual custom to choose the Lord Mayor from each of the two parties alternately, irrespective of the swings of opinion; and a common, though not invariable, practice to see that each of the Council's Committees has a Chairman drawn from one party and a Vice-Chairman from the other. This is frequently remarked on by visitors from other towns as a sensible arrangement. The municipal politics of Leicester have indeed been conducted, on the whole, in a civilised fashion.

Outside the Council violence erupts, here as elsewhere, from time to time. But even the most emotionally explosive issue, of alien immigration, though it has led to street fights and occasional demonstrations, has produced no murderous disorders like that in Nottingham in 1958. Not yet, that is: the atmosphere began to become thundery in September 1972 as a result of the crisis in Uganda; and protest may well take one of the hatefully prevalent forms of violence.

Or one might choose another example. In February 1968, as in a number of other British universities, there was disorder for the better part of a week in the University of Leicester, arising from a demand put forward by students for a greater share in their government. The University (conveniently situated in the middle of the country) became the *venue* of a whole series of protests concerning the affairs of other institutions far distant from Leicester. The argument was angry, and seared a mark on the University that will not be effaced. But it led to an agreement, which has been found to work with reasonable satisfaction since and was achieved without the physical violence that disrupted the London School of Economics and appeared in its worst forms in Paris and the United States.

And finally it should be noted that although, in Leicester as in most other similar places, professional football has induced rowdy disturbance, it has been kept here within bounds. The fans make a nasty exhibition of themselves, in trains and elsewhere, from time to time; but they have never, even for a moment, made the name of Leicester a byword for barbarity, as they have sometimes made the name of Liverpool and – outstandingly – of Glasgow. This too in years when Leicester City has reached the Cup Final on three occasions (1961, 1963, 1969), to be defeated every time.

So that the old moderation, the absence of embattled conflict, that we have noted repeatedly in the long history of Leicester continues to characterise the city, even when violence has become a commonplace, a fashionable cult in the world at large. That should not be a cause for complacency. It is a generalisation that may be upset at any time, in some horrible fashion. But it has been the business of this book to consider the past, and that immediate past which we are apt loosely to call the present; and it is fair to the city to record that, up to the time when these words were printed, it remained true to a long and honourable tradition.

7

In 1960 no one could have predicted, accurately and comprehensively, what Leicester would be like by 1970. Political, economic, technological developments have all taken, at some points, an unexpected course. If a forecast were attempted here, it would turn out no less false. One prophecy can nevertheless be made, not indeed with certainty but with a good deal of confidence. Whether the problems of central Leicester, the historic town, are solved or not, the whole urban entity of which it is the heart will continue to grow. It is time now to consider the formation of that entity, the development of Greater Leicester.

IV
Greater Leicester

I

The outstanding fact in the recent history of Leicester is the fact of physical expansion. That expansion did not begin at any one moment; nor is it attributable to one cause. It becomes apparent, something that can be demonstrated and measured, towards the end of the eighteenth century. In the nineteenth it becomes conspicuous. The fastest growth occurred in the 1860s, and in commenting on it, the Census Commissioners remarked that although 'houses are being rapidly built, and are no sooner finished than they are occupied', this physical expansion was still taking place almost entirely within the boundaries of the borough. 'There is a small extension beyond the municipal limits', they observed, 'but this is mainly by the erection of villa-residences, occupied by the employers of labour.'[1] In the next twenty years things changed, and in 1892 that was recognised by an extension of the boundaries of the County Borough, to include substantial parts of the six ancient parishes adjoining it. Four of those parishes – Aylestone, Evington, Braunstone and Humberstone – had been entirely rural, showing no significant increase of population before 1871: there were fewer people in Aylestone then than there had been thirty years earlier. Belgrave was easily the largest of the six, and the only one much affected by industry. The population grew by over a quarter in the 1860s, and the Census Commissioners attributed the increase specifically to the proximity of the village to Leicester. The sixth parish, Knighton, had always been suburban, a chapelry of St Margaret's in the town; and though it too was still very rural in the main, Leicester had long been overflowing gently across its northern borders. A well-informed gazetteer of the 1860s remarks of it that 'many of the houses are villas, with large gardens, and inhabited by the manu-facturers of Leicester'.[2]

[1] pp. 1872 lxvi, pt. ii, 344.
[2] Wilson, *Imperial Gazetteer*, i. 1136.

After 1870, however, all this changed. In the next decade the population of Aylestone and Belgrave doubled; in 1881–91 it doubled again in Aylestone, trebled in Knighton, and rose by nearly 60 per cent in Belgrave.[1] The boundary change of 1892 took place exactly at the moment when the growth of the County Borough was beginning to slacken. Had that change not occurred, the population would have increased by only 16 per cent in the previous decade – nearly the slowest rate of growth at any time since the census was first taken.

What was beginning to happen in Leicester in the 1880s has gone much further since. Today the population of the city usually falls from one year's estimate to the next, until it receives an artificial increase by another extension of boundaries. But the boundary, however drawn, is a misleading one, which does not coincide with the whole urban complex that must, in modern conditions, be regarded as the true city. For there is a Greater Leicester, whose population is relentlessly increasing at the perimeter, while it is stationary or declining at the heart. The phenomenon is in no way peculiar to Leicester. It is common to most of the large old towns in Britain and in the whole Western world. Here, on the evidence of the census figures, we recognise its emergence with some precision. Greater Leicester, as we know it today, came into existence in 1871–91.

What caused the change? In some towns, in London for example, in Nottingham and Birmingham, it could be attributed largely to improvements in transport: to the building of suburban railways, to the horse-drawn bus and tram. None of these things was equally important in Leicester. There were never more than two railway stations there that could truly be called suburban – stations, that is, built to serve outlying districts of the town, not separate villages adjoining, like Glenfield or Wigston Magna. Both these stations lay on the Humberstone Road. The first, half a mile north of the main Midland station, was not opened until 1875. It promptly became quite busy, and was a good investment for the company. The other, on the Great Northern line, was opened in 1883 and never of much value to any one.[2]

The contrast here between Leicester and Nottingham is striking.[3] In Nottingham the Town Council attached so much importance to suburban railway development that it obtained statutory power to invest in a railway company, promoted for the purpose in 1886. When the Manchester Sheffield & Lincolnshire Railway secured its Act for building a grand new main line through both towns, Nottingham required it to open four stations, besides its large central one, within the

[1] VCHL iii. 179, note *e*.
[2] See the Midland Company's station statistics in British Transport Historical Records, MID 4/1–6. No figures of this kind are available in respect of the other railway companies serving Leicester.
[3] Cf. *The Victorian City*, ed. Dyos and Wolff, i. 289–92, 299.

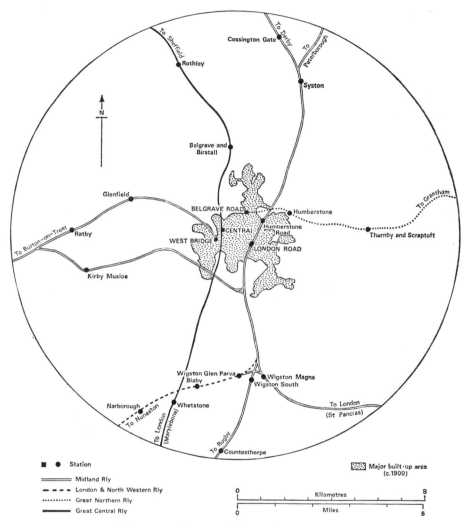

Leicester railways within a five-mile radius

borough boundaries, and to guarantee them an adequate service. In Leicester the Council showed no concern whatever in this matter. It was content to see only one suburban station on the new line, at Belgrave, barely within the boundary; and to allow the railway to pass close to the centre of Aylestone (where there were already 5,400 people by 1891) without providing a station – though in 1899 it tried to persuade the Midland company to open a station to serve that suburb.[1]

[1] *Council Minutes*, 1898–9, 223; 1899–1900, 213–14.

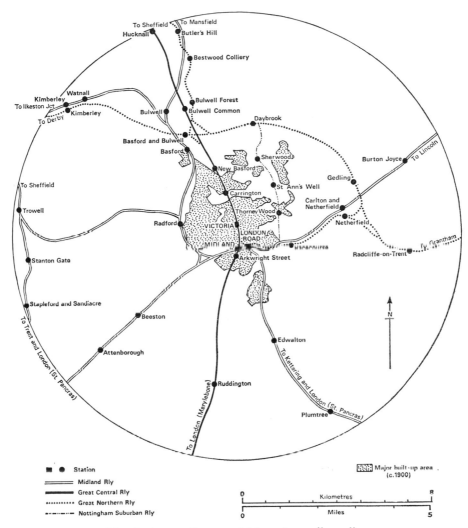

Nottingham railways within a five-mile radius

As for other means of transport, they were all horse-drawn. If the steam tram had succeeded better when it was tried on the Belgrave Road in 1876, and had been adopted permanently, it might have played as useful a part in Leicester as it did in Birmingham. As it was, the tramways remained unmechanised until 1904: though it is right to remember that the horse-operated system was carrying nearly 11 million passengers annually at its end, and a sizeable proportion of them must have been travelling in from the terminal points of the system to their daily work in Leicester. The horse-tram service certainly provided one induce-ment to those who might think of going to live in Stoneygate or Clarendon Park or on the Narborough Road; but that was only one among a number of others. Though improved transport undoubtedly helped to produce the change we are discussing, it was not the sole cause of it, nor the most important one.

We can see it also in terms of health and amenity. In the course of the Victorian age the Old Town came to be almost entirely abandoned as a residential district.[1] Warned repeatedly by Sanitary Commissioners and Medical Officers of Health, those who could afford it removed from the proximity of the river. Mills and factories, then for the first time coming to be erected in substantial numbers, dis-placed houses. For the poor, that simply meant eviction, with the need to find other quarters; quarters perhaps, for the time being, even more overcrowded and insanitary than those that had been demolished. For the more prosperous, how-ever, new possibilities were now opening up in streets being built in the 1850s and 1860s – off the Belgrave Road or Braunstone Gate, for example, or in the High-fields. The well-to-do were erecting villas for themselves, detached or in pairs. The London Road hill is crowned by two dating from 1876–7; and by that time the development of Stoneygate, beyond the Victoria Park, was in full swing. But Stoneygate comprises much more than the imposing houses, built for manu-facturers and professional men, on the London Road. It might almost be called a middle-class town on its own, in microcosm, with the associated streets of smaller houses leading off to the north of the main road, and the quarter known as Claren-don Park to the south. There was accommodation here for the whole range of society from the wealthiest citizen in the town to the plain artisan; though, neither then nor now, anything resembling a slum. And by the end of the century the district was practically self-contained, with all the conveniences that could reason-ably be sought for: shops in Queen's Road, schools (St John's, 1890; Avenue Road Board School, 1894), a public library – the Knighton branch, opened in 1896 on land given by the owners of the Clarendon Park Estate, was one of the first to be established in the territory added to the borough by the boundary extension.[2] Only one amenity was absent: nowhere in the district was there a single public house. There is only one now.

By such developments, and by ribbon-building along the main roads, each of the six parishes incorporated in part with Leicester in 1892 had come by the end of the century to be almost continuously connected with the town. Yet they all remained,

[1] The population of St Martin's parish fell at every census after 1811; that of All Saints' and of the Liberty of the Newarke grew very little after 1861.
[2] M. Seaborne, *Recent Education from Local Sources* (1967), 11–16; Libraries Committee, 24 *Report* (1894–5) 8; 25 *Report* (1895–6) 5.

in a greater or less degree, village communities until the First World War and beyond. Let us look at them a little more closely.[1]

2

By this date none of them had a resident lord of the manor, though all still contained at least one substantial gentleman's house: Belgrave, Evington, and Humberstone each had two, Aylestone, Braunstone, and Knighton one. In Aylestone development had been expedited by the Duke of Rutland's decision to sell the manor at auction in 1869. Hitherto he had been sole landowner; now the estate was split up into small lots. None of his family had lived in Aylestone Hall for very many years; appropriately, the occupying tenant who bought it was a land agent.[2] The change that followed was swift. It affected especially the northern part of the parish, which became in all respects a suburb of Leicester under the name of Aylestone Park.

In Aylestone, then, change came when a rich absentee landlord sold his property. The rich absentee had also figured in the village's history in another sense for a long time past. The living was one of the best in the county, and in the gift of the Earls and Dukes of Rutland. In the eighteenth century and the early nineteenth the rectors were usually non-resident, and the parish was served by curates. Cobbett treats us to a vigorous diatribe against one of the Rectors of Aylestone (Gilbert Beresford) on this account.[3] The rectors had maintained an imposing house for themselves (in the seventeenth century it seems to have been slightly bigger than the Hall). When Beresford rebuilt it in 1839, it was an indication of change in the prevailing ideas of churchmanship.[4]

Aylestone and Belgrave were the only two of these six parishes that lay on the river. When the Soar was canalised in 1791 artificial cuts were made on both sides of Belgrave, where it could not be rendered navigable; and when the communication was carried on southward Aylestone became the point at which the artificial waterway emerged from the river. Both parishes preserved medieval bridges, and indeed preserve them still: the Aylestone one a packhorse bridge, standing out in isolation now in the meadows, that at Belgrave enlarged, but not reconstructed, to carry the traffic of a turnpike road.

[1] The history of these parishes is dealt with succinctly in VCHL iv. 415–28, 434–46.
[2] *Ibid.*, iv. 419.
[3] *Rural Rides* (Everyman edn.), ii. 266–7.
[4] Beresford had been the non-resident rector from 1813 to 1820. He had then ceded the living to Henry Browne, but he returned to it in 1838, and the rebuilding of the rectory indicates plainly his intention of residing there He died in 1843. M. P. Dare, *Aylestone Manor and Church* (1924), 65.

It must have been at least in part owing to these good communications that Belgrave became the first of the five villages to be industrialised. By 1851 nearly a quarter of the population was engaged in framework knitting. The work was mostly domestic, but there were three stockingers' shops. The suburbanisation of that part of the parish close to the main road went on; gas lighting appeared in 1864. The other four parishes remained almost entirely agricultural until their expansion began late in the nineteenth century. Knighton continued to be the most genteel and secluded. In the 1830s, unlike all the others, it had no tradesmen or shops of any kind, and neither public house nor beer shop – in contrast to Aylestone, which had four, and to Humberstone, where there were three, together with such tradesmen as bakers and blacksmiths.[1]

Though none of these places could be called distinguished, each had something special of its own. At Evington the triangular green, with the houses grouped around it, was a delightful example of one familiar type of English village, graced unusually by a pretty little Gothic chapel of 1838, with the Minister's house adjoining. The parish church has a striking north aisle, with an image of the patron saint in a niche on the eastern gable and window tracery of uncommon and interesting design (Plate 23b). At Aylestone the chancel, 'splendidly tall and long',[2] is appropriate to the church of a rich rectory; and one of the rich rectors himself is commemorated by a large Elizabethan brass. Humberstone church stands up sturdily on the slope above the village, with its bulky tower and squat steeple. The body of it was almost entirely rebuilt in 1857–8, and the work was well done, with a delicate and rare use of alabaster. The architect was Raphael Brandon, who was subsequently employed in Leicester itself on the new spire of St Martin's.

The Halls at Knighton and Belgrave have already been discussed in another connection (i.100, 140). At Belgrave the Hall and the House faced each other across 'the Gravel', an informal enclosure terminated at one end by the parish church in its shady churchyard and at the other by a noble elm. Even before the motor-car arrived it was a haven of peace from the clatter of traffic up and down the Loughborough Road, 100 yards away.

Finally, it is worth recalling that three men of distinction came from these villages on the edge of Leicester. John Paget, son of Thomas Paget of Humberstone and born there in 1811, produced in *The New Examen* the most powerful critique of Macaulay's *History of England* that we have yet seen. Knighton Hall was the early home of two notable men. Joseph Cradock was born, almost certainly in the house, in 1741. His kindliness and public spirit have already appeared (i.120, 124). They irradiate his long *Memoirs* too. Discursive and often fussy, the book yet reflects very well the mind and temper of a cultivated gentleman, who

[1] *Pigot & Co.'s Directory* (1835), 126–37.
[2] Pevsner, *Buildings of England: Leicestershire and Rutland*, 167.

moved in the best literary society of London. Charles Adderley, 1st Lord Norton, born at Knighton Hall in 1814, influenced British colonial policy and was President of the Board of Trade in Disraeli's Government of 1874. He played a notable part in the planning and development of eastern Birmingham.

3

The extension of the boundaries of Leicester in 1892 aroused some opposition. It was the second attempt – a previous one had been made in 1886, and failed; and it had a particular interest as one of the first major boundary changes to be brought forward in which the two most powerful entities created by the Local Government Act of 1888, County Borough and County Council, came into conflict. Not that the new Leicestershire Council was wholly opposed to the change. It accepted the validity of the principle on which the proposal was based: the need to bring the urban fringes of Leicester under the same administration as that of the county borough, with which they now were, or were becoming, economically united. Between these two bodies the battle centred, as we should expect, on the issue of rateable value. No procedure had yet been laid down for determining if compensation, in any form, might be due to one authority yielding territory to another. Hence, in large part, the protracted and wearisome arguments conducted before the Committee of the House of Commons charged with scrutinising the Bill.[1] In the end there was, of course, compromise. Leicester had started out by trying to secure the incorporation of almost the whole of the six parishes. It got something much less: nearly all Aylestone and most of Belgrave, a third of Knighton and Evington, a quarter of Humberstone, together with a seventh of Braunstone, which was historically a chapelry of Glenfield.

In these communities themselves, opinion was a good deal divided. In Belgrave, for example, whilst the Local Board petitioned against the change, the School Board and the Burial Board welcomed it. In the end the borough was able to show that approval had been expressed by the owners of more than three-quarters of the property concerned.[2] Those who objected could not reasonably do so on the grounds that they would be compelled to pay higher rates: for the rates in the borough were in general lower. It was fair to argue that transfer to the borough would be likely to bring some better services, particularly through the extension of the municipal gas and water supplies. On the other hand, the opponents of the change contended strenuously that Leicester had not yet purged itself of the

[1] House of Lords Record Office: Minutes of Evidence of Commons Committee on Private Bills (Group B) 1891, vols. 126–7, 3–12 March 1891. Cf. also Storey, 145–70.
[2] Evidence cited in previous note: vol. 126, table, 4 March.

Parish and Borough Boundaries

misconduct of its drainage works and sewerage (12–14), and that those who were outside its boundaries would do better to stay there until that task had been achieved. One can sympathise with Alderman Thomas Wright, who bore the brunt of defending the proposals before the Commons Committee under cross-questioning by F. T. D. Ledgard, Q.C., a particularly offensive example of his kind, who represented the Leicestershire County Council: for the County Council had had no problems whatever of this intractable sort to solve. But it is nevertheless true that here the objectors had good ground for disquiet.

In the end, the borough prevailed on almost every essential point. The argument about compensation was ultimately decided by the arbitration of the Local Government Board, which the county had vehemently rejected when the town proposed it; and the areas, as finally decided, suited the interests of Leicester very well. On the whole it seems fair to conclude that they also suited the interests of the people affected by them.

Alderman Wright's services to his town were handsomely recognised. An entirely new Council had to be formed when the Extension Act came into force, and he was at once elected Mayor. In the same year he was appointed an honorary freeman; he was knighted in 1893 (Plate 12). He was saluted as the 'first Mayor of Greater Leicester'.[1]

4

The extension of 1892 brought nearly 33,000 people into the county borough, increased its area by more than a third and its rateable value by about a fifth. But a change of boundaries could be, at first, little more than a paper transaction. What would be done to knead the new parts of the borough and the old into a single whole?

The first determined attempt to profit by the change was made in the northern part of the old parish of Evington. There a Leicester architect, Arthur Wakerley, had been buying land since 1885. He must have done so in anticipation of the enlargement of the borough that was then contemplated. He had a special purpose in mind, to create something like a new community. It was to be, frankly, a suburb, for the residence of people working in Leicester: not unified, like the Saltaire of the 1850s or the contemporary Bournville, by the ownership of a single employer with his works adjacent; nor a satellite town, surrounded by a green belt, such as Ebenezer Howard sketched out in 1898 and began to realise at Letchworth in 1903. Wakerley's mind was not adventurous. He had no notion of trying to separate industrial and residential development; he encouraged the establishment of factories as far as he could. But he did sincerely aim at producing a suburb with important merits that most existing suburbs lacked. He wished to provide it with its own services, so that it should not be commercially dependent on the town it adjoined; and to make of it a coherent community, which should generate a life of its own.

At the boundary extension of 1892, Wakerley's North Evington was brought into Leicester easily, for it was separated from the old village by an ample tract of open country. In the year in which the measure came into force a market square

[1] Storey, 165.

was laid out there (which Wakerley presented to the borough) with a market hall. So the work went on, until by 1914 the district was almost completely built up. It was a suburb well in advance of the general run of such places. In terms of land ownership and society, it was very different from the other suburb we have considered, Stoneygate. They had however one thing in common, characteristic of Nonconformist Leicester. Under Wakerley's direction North Evington too was wholly without public houses.

Wakerley's was not the only experimental development in these years. Side by side with his work, a scheme for a Garden Suburb went forward, on lines different from his. It was an offshoot of a co-operative manufacturing firm, the Anchor Boot & Shoe Productive Society, founded in 1893. Following an example set in Ealing, a co-operative housing venture known as Anchor Tenants Ltd was established, which acquired seventeen acres of land adjoining Keyham Lane, directly east of the old village of Humberstone, in 1907. This was proudly called a Garden Suburb, and it had some small claim to the title, though doubtless Ebenezer Howard would have rejected it. By 1915 there were 350 people living there, in ninety-five houses. The Suburb also included three shops, rooms for meetings and recreation, tennis courts and a bowling green, and it achieved some real sense of community. Gas and water were laid on, but not – it is to be noted – main sewerage or electricity. Perhaps the chief drawback to living in the Suburb lay in its unsatisfactory transport. The Anchor factory, where most of the tenants worked, was over two miles to the south, across the grain of the roads and railway. Getting into Leicester and out of it was also tiresome until an enterprising tenant started a bus service to feed the Corporation trams, a mile and more away on the Humberstone Road. The Garden Suburb was overtaken by the war and then by much larger developments in public housing; but it was a brave endeavour, and it certainly offered the conditions for a much better life than many of the close-packed Victorian streets near the middle of the town.[1]

5

The boundary of the borough that was established in 1892 was defensible as a political compromise. It did not remain valid for long as in any sense an expression of the true limits of the town. We have noted that as early as the 1880s the expansion of Leicester itself was slowing up. Some of the neighbouring villages, however – other than those now taken partly into the borough – were growing to a substantial size. Wigston Magna had always been the biggest of them. In 1801 it

[1] The history of the Garden Suburb is told by G. C. Martin in *The Growth of Leicester*, ed. Brown, 79–82.

had exceeded Lutterworth in population and fell not far short of Melton Mowbray. By 1901 it contained 8,400 people. During that century it had gone through great tribulation.[1] The old agricultural economy had broken up, giving place chiefly to the hosiery manufacture, with the pitifully low wages that industry offered. The diversification that did so much to improve conditions of employment in Leicester arrived here very late, with the building of the railways (three lines converged on South Wigston) and some factories that came to be conveniently sited on them. But it was on a much smaller scale, and it clearly benefited Wigston much less. By 1900 the growth of the place had halted, not to be resumed for a quarter of a century. Towards the close of the Victorian age one can discern the first signs of the end of its old independence. In the past it had had little to do with Leicester, except as a market and as the distributive centre of the hosiery trade. Now we can see Wigston people beginning to move in and out of Leicester for their daily work. The two Midland Railway stations handled some 110,000 passengers a year between them, together with over 500 season-ticket holders, most of whom must have been travelling to and from Leicester.[2]

If the population of Wigston was now stationary, some of the other villages were growing fast. Narborough doubled in size in 1901–11, Rothley and Oadby both increased by half. The growth of Oadby is particularly striking. It might have been much greater if the horse tramway had been extended out from Leicester to Oadby church, under powers granted in 1884.[3] As it was, the village had no railway station of its own, and no tram nearer than the borough boundary, a mile from its centre. The electrification of that tram route in 1904 must have stimulated expansion, of which some of the memorials are visible today in the big houses lying on and near Stoughton Drive South and Manor Road (Plate 22a), the successors to those built in Stoneygate by the prosperous business men of Leicester of the preceding generation.

There was, then, growth in these years in some of the smaller communities surrounding the borough, standstill in others. But in general, with the exceptions that have been noted and always remembering the ancient permeation of the villages by domestic industry, we can say that Leicester was still girdled round, quite close in, by open agricultural country. In 1911 the population of those districts that lay outside the county borough boundary but adjoined it was about 34,000 – almost exactly the same number as had been taken into the borough in 1891. It may be worth adding here, as a portent for the future, that it was now, at the census of 1911, that Leicester attained its highest point of growth in relation to Leicestershire. In 1801 the population of the borough had been 13 per cent of

[1] Recounted with feeling in W. G. Hoskins, *The Midland Peasant* (1957), chap. x.
[2] British Transport Historical Records: MID 4/1–6.
[3] Storey, 172.

that of the county; in 1911 it was 47.6 per cent. By 1971 it had fallen to about 37 per cent.

The First World War restricted the movement of population and the pattern of economic enterprise. Even before it began the shortage of houses was giving concern to the Town Council, and as soon as it was over a serious effort was made to repair the deficiency (see p. 67). It soon became clear that the city would have to seek land for building houses well outside its boundaries, and in 1925 it purchased most of the manor of Braunstone for this purpose. A prerequisite of any such development was satisfactory public transport. This need was met by the Corporation's new motor-buses (not by trams) – to Saffron Lane, for example, in 1925, to Braunstone Lane in 1928 – supplemented by services developed by the largest of the private operators, the Midland Red Company.

At the same time houses were being built by private enterprise on a large scale, most of them beyond the municipal boundary. This was very striking to the north, where the population of the three adjacent parishes of Birstall, Thurmaston, and Syston doubled in 1921–31; but on the south side Wigston, after a long stagnation, also grew by 28 per cent, Oadby by 46 per cent. All these old villages were situated on main roads; and much of the private housing of these years was in the form of ribbon development along them. Municipal housing was not of that kind – except here and there, as on Saffron Lane and Knighton Lane East, which developed in time some of the characteristics of main highways. The pattern was conspicuously exemplified at Oadby, where a by-pass was built in 1930 to take the heavy traffic on the A6 clear of the old village, and that was almost immediately lined with suburban houses. It was already coming to be recognised, however, that this was a deplorable practice, and there is no other instance of it so flagrant anywhere in the neighbourhood of Leicester.

Many people now began to seek houses further afield, outside the borough boundaries; and that became easier for the well-to-do through the development of the motor vehicle. The prosperous business man, when he established a family home in the 1920s, could feel free to do so anywhere within motoring distance of his work in Leicester – say at Rothley or beyond, on the fringes of Charwood Forest. Those large houses, not long built, at Oadby were now *vieux jeu*: the largest of them not least because they included stables, with quarters for a coachman and grooms, where now all that was needed was a garage. The social consequences for Leicester itself were, as we have seen, important. The car's counterpart in public transport, the motor-bus, wrought its change more slowly. Although in the 1920s a system of bus routes came to be established with Leicester as their centre, the scale on which they operated was as yet small. In 1931 the census revealed no more than 6,615 people as coming into Leicester for their daily work from places of residence outside. Still, this was the start of a great expansion. Twenty years later that number had multiplied more than four times over.[1]

The extension of the municipal boundary in 1935 was, in many respects, a logical continuation of the one made forty years earlier. Virtually all of Belgrave, Evington, and Humberstone that had remained outside the city was now included within it. The whole northern part of Braunstone was transferred, to bring the new housing estate inside the city boundary. The dividing line ran along the north side of Braunstone Lane, which left over 4,000 of the parishioners still in the county. Braunstone Frith (which had been a separate civil parish since 1857) now passed to Leicester: an acquisition valuable not in terms of population – in 1931 that was seven – but because it included what was intended to be the municipal airport. It fulfilled that function in scarcely more than a nominal sense until 1939; and when the war was over most of it was laid out as a golf course.

But the changes of 1935 were less rational than those of 1892; determined just as clearly by a political contest, chiefly – though not solely – between the City and County Councils. They could not be said to correspond in any sense to the economic or social realities of urban or rural life. The new boundary cut Birstall in two; it ran right up to Anstey and yet left it outside; at Glenfield it stopped short of a large new housing development that was actually under way, and purely suburban in character. It corresponded neither to the existing state of the society, nor to its history, nor to any physical divisions. Yet it cannot be dismissed as unimportant, something merely drawn on a map, for it was a dividing line between services, which might – in such a matter as the collection of household refuse, for example – affect people's lives very intimately. The County Council had by now been in existence for nearly half a century; and, after a necessarily slow start, it had developed its own services, separately and at some points differently from those established in the City.

The City and County Education Committees, both guided by energetic Directors (F. P. Armitage for Leicester, W. E. Brockington for Leicestershire), were entirely reorganising the structure of elementary education in these years, working towards the abolition of the older type of school, where children of all ages were taught (often by a single teacher), in favour of separate senior schools, whether 'grammar' or 'modern'. The first of the separate schools in the county was at Enderby. By 1939, 93 per cent of the county schools had been treated in this way. Leicestershire, though by no means a rich authority, had moved in this matter in the vanguard of a policy of genuine progress. Much of that policy has now been reversed, owing partly to changed conditions and partly to new fashions in educational doctrine. But it was on the foundation of Brockington's work that

[1] *Census of* 1951. *England and Wales. Report on usual Residences and Workplaces* (1956), 121.

the much-publicised Leicestershire Plan, promulgated by his successor, was reared,[1] to produce a marked divergence from the practice adopted in the City. That did not become glaring until the 1950s. But already, before the Second World War, there were differences in educational outlook and facilities. The location of schools was beginning to become, for some parents, a factor of importance in deciding whether to live within the City boundary or beyond it.

In other relations of life the differences might be more striking. No library service whatever was provided by the County Council until 1922; and then it did not develop fast. The City Reference Library and its Newspaper Room were open, as they had been from the outset in 1871, freely to all comers; but a resident outside the municipal boundary had to pay an annual fee if he wished to borrow, and – more important – he had to come into the City, to the Central Lending Library or one of its branches, to fetch his books. If he depended on public transport, that might be expensive. The trams and buses of the Corporation operated only inside the boundary. Beyond it, the field was left to private companies. The Corporation system, a tight network, was efficiently managed, and the fares ruling on it were low. The private operators had in many respects a more difficult task: a dispersed chain of routes, some of them through thinly-peopled country, which could never yield a revenue comparable with those in the City. As a natural consequence, they provided an infrequent service, and charged relatively high fares. All this is intelligible, given the existence of the administrative boundary and the firm determination of the municipality to operate its own public transport. But by the 1930s it was beginning to exasperate those who were chiefly affected by it, residents living a little beyond the boundary – that is, towards the outer edge of the Greater Leicester that was emerging. Though people were more willing to walk then than they are now, a long, wet, windy mile of road separated the centre of Oadby from the Stoneygate tram terminus. As Oadby developed in these years, a great part of the new residents worked in Leicester. It seemed more and more illogical and tiresome that they should have to put up with a sparse, expensive transport service, when a frequent and cheap one was available across the frontier.

Nor did the arrangement affect only those who travelled daily to work in Leicester. All the large-scale development of retail trade in these years was to be found at the centre of the City: the three old-established firms of drapers, now grown into department stores; the multiple grocers, who could often undersell the village shops, which were all that Blaby or Thurmaston could offer. Above all, there was the market, still drawing in as it had always done the business of the rural districts, but an equally strong magnet for the suburbs. These were the chief forces that gave unity to Greater Leicester. The unity was often frustrated, however, by the anomalous urban boundary.

[1] 43 TLAS (1967–8) 56.

6

Such were a few of the difficulties arising from the administrative division, as they appeared to people living in Greater Leicester between the Wars. They were equally, perhaps more, disturbing to those who were responsible for the government of the whole district; and as the concept of planning grew stronger on a national and regional scale, in terms of the Barlow, Scott, and Uthwatt Reports of 1940–2 and all that succeeded them, they stood out more conspicuously still. It became clear beyond mistake that the structure of local government established in 1888 would have to be substantially modified.

The relation between Leicester and Leicestershire afforded in many ways almost a clinical specimen of the problem at large. Historically, it had been established for a thousand years. On the surface, it seemed to be accepted almost as a condition of life – or at least like the weather, as something English, irrational, ordained and unchangeable. The peculiar conditions of the relationship here made it seem, in a special degree, natural. What did perhaps most to destroy its equilibrium was the growth of Greater Leicester.

The growth continued relentlessly when the second war was over and the normal pressures of peaceful life could be exerted. In 1951–65 the population of Leicester and its district grew by over 18,000 as a result of migration – an increase twice as large as that in the corresponding district of Nottingham. In 1951 the district included 442,000 people. By 1965 there were 505,000.[1]

As in nearly all other towns of the same sort in Great Britain, this growth took place almost entirely in the outlying parts of the district, and was accompanied – though by no means counterbalanced – by a fall in the resident population of the city, within its administrative boundary. That population reached another peak, of 283,540, in 1966, when a minor adjustment of the boundary took place, which brought some 16,000 more people into the city; but again thereafter the population fell.

In physical terms this process was obvious, in the large areas of open space, where houses had been demolished, within a half-mile radius of the Clock Tower: to the point where strangers to the city sometimes supposed that it must have suffered severely from air-raids and that the damage was very slow to be repaired. The City Council was, however, attempting to reverse this long-established trend. Profiting by the spectacle of many American cities, it committed itself to large

[1] *The East Midlands Study* (1966), 17, 117. This 'Leicester District' does not correspond to 'Greater Leicester' as described below, pp. 131–3. It embraces a larger area, described on p. 109 of the *Study*.

schemes of housing development on cleared sites near the centre (cf. pp. 91–3)
But though, by such expedients, something was being done to adjust the balance of
development, it did not, in terms of gross figures, alter the established pattern. In
other vital respects the old city centre retained its primacy. It continued to be the
commercial headquarters of the whole district, the capital of its retail trade: with
the result that the rapidly-growing outer districts poured more and more people,
as each year went by, into the Market Place and the streets converging on the
Clock Tower. Nor was it shopping alone that attracted them. Leicester City had
only one ground, in Filbert Street; the Tigers and County Cricket drew in their
thousands too. It was reasonable that these things should be established near the
focal point of the whole urban complex. But the road system was not built to carry
the traffic thus engendered, and every one suffered accordingly.

Watching these developments in recent years, one has at times a despairing sense
of the irresistible triumph of the motor-car. If on a Saturday one observes what is
happening near the centre, it is as if one were at the vortex of a whirlpool. Not
many of the cars are crossing the city, for great efforts have been made to divert
through traffic by Charles Street and Vaughan Way and the ring roads. Most of
them, it is quite plain, are bringing people into the centre for shopping or amenities,
their drivers preoccupied with the problem of finding a place to park – making
inadequate use of the Corporation Transport Department's effort to ease their
difficulties by providing a 'Park'n Ride' service, of frequent buses from large car
parks to the centre. In the long run, this free-for-all cannot continue. But it has
been one of the accepted conditions of living in Greater Leicester in the past
twenty years. The Leicester Traffic Plan threw out a ringing challenge in 1964:
'*This is the dilemma: the city centre or the motor-car*'.[1] The challenge still goes
unanswered.

What has happened at the perimeter to counteract this force? Perhaps rather
more than is commonly realised. For many years past, the chief development of
factories and warehouses has been far away from the centre: along the Melton
Road, towards Thurmaston and beyond it; on the Hinckley and Narborough
Roads, and at Wigston. The Leicester Permanent Building Society set an important example in 1964, when it removed its headquarters to a large new building, employing 330 people there. Some of the outer districts have developed
substantial shopping centres of their own. One of them, on Aikman Avenue in the
New Parks Estate, secured a bronze medal from the Royal Institute of British
Architects, as the outstanding building erected in the Leicester and Rutland
Province in the years 1950–7.[2]

Another interesting development in retail trade has been the establishment of

---

[1] *Leicester Traffic Plan*, 65.
[2] LM 2 January 1959.

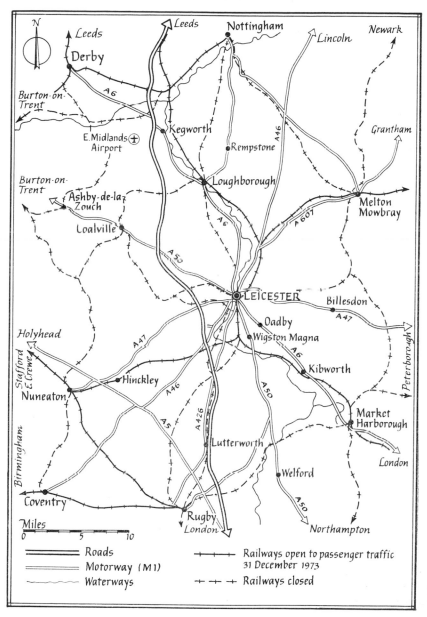

Communications in 1974

Woolco at Oadby and Waitrose on Ethel Road, below the General Hospital. These were early ventures of their kind in Britain, though the type was already well known in the United States: of the large department or provision store near the outer edge of a big urban district. They can serve residents in the immediate locality (there are nearly 50,000 of them in the Urban Districts of Oadby and Wigston alone) and at the same time draw in people from south and east Leicestershire who would otherwise go down to swell the congestion round the Clock Tower. Equally, they can – and they do – attract custom from the city itself, in easy traffic conditions and with the comfortable expectation of parking space.

Again and again, in Leicester as in so many other cities, one can see transport as a factor of overriding importance: an importance that would have appeared quite disproportionate in any analysis of the kind made fifty years ago. It has its peculiarities here. The contribution of the railways to suburban development in Leicester was always, as we have seen, small. In recent years it has been eliminated altogether, through a combination of the relentless advance of the motor vehicle and the deliberate policy of the Railways Board, unchecked by any intervention from the central Government. Twenty years ago there were seventeen stations within a five-mile radius of Leicester. Those twenty were reduced to one – until in 1970, after a long argument, Narborough was re-opened with a minimal service in the morning and evening. Why Narborough alone, one might ask? Syston did more business, Sileby much more;[1] but they were closed and demolished. The explanation is purely technical: that they lay on a high-speed main line, from which it was convenient to remove all stopping traffic. That answer merely emphasises the insignificance of the local passengers as compared with those moving through on their way from London to Sheffield. It has been responsibly suggested that it may well be necessary to reinstate some of the suburban services that have been lost in and around Leicester, and to invigorate them as never before, as a cheaper alternative to the building of monorail systems or the limitless enlargement of roads.[2]

The journey to work presents in some respects less formidable problems in Leicester than in some other towns. A relatively large number of those who are employed in the Leicester area also reside there: among office workers, a higher proportion than in Nottingham, a much higher proportion than in Derby.[3]

[1] C. Sharp, *Problems of Urban Passenger Transport* (1967), 99.
[2] *Ibid.*, 102–3.
[3] *Office Services in the East Midlands*, 237.

7

Although it is plain that a 'Greater Leicester' has come into being in the course of the past century, there is no agreement about the meaning of the phrase, in a geographical, economic, or social sense.[1] Obviously, it may be applied to the total continuous built-up area, which stretches at the present time from Birstall to Oadby along the A6, from Kirby Muxloe and Leicester Forest East along the A47 to Bushby. But that definition is not useful. It ceases to be valid as soon as a new cluster of houses is built on the perimeter, and as it does not correspond to any administrative boundary it is difficult to adopt for even the simplest statistical purpose. Moreover, 'Greater Leicester' is a term that can be usefully employed for something larger and more complicated than a mere collection of contiguous buildings. It should express economic and social functions, which may affect people living further out, beyond the continuous built-up area, just as much as those within it. Something better than this is needed.

The *Leicester Traffic Plan* of 1964 made use of a definition of Greater Leicester for its own purposes, within a 'cordon line', which was unfortunately delineated only on a small-scale map.[2] The *East Midlands Study*, however, produced by the Economic Planning Council of the Region in 1966, was more specific. Here the boundaries were drawn simply, and very widely, to produce a Leicester District – 'the area we may call Greater Leicester' – taking in Loughborough, the Urban Districts of Oadby, Wigston, and Shepshed, and the Rural Districts of Barrow-on-Soar, Billesdon, and Blaby.[3] These existing units of local government were adopted *en bloc*: no attempt was made to discriminate between those parts of them that were linked closely to Leicester and those that were orientated elsewhere. The inclusion of Loughborough was surely a mistake. For a town of 40,000 people it has a quite marked independence, an inward-looking character of its own deriving largely from its industrial structure and from the accident, which it sensibly exploits – as it has often done in the past – that it is roughly equidistant from Leicester, Derby, and Nottingham. It is within Leicester's orbit for some purposes; but for others it stands on its own, or looks to its northern neighbours.

Two other serious attempts have been made to define 'Greater Leicester' since, in planning studies undertaken by the City and County Councils jointly, in 1969 and 1972. The earlier of them produced a much more restricted definition, to

[1] The confusion is well exemplified in *Region*, where 'Greater Leicester' appears with two totally different boundaries (neither of them explained) on pp. 457 and 598.
[2] p. 9.
[3] pp. 17, 109.

Greater Leicester

include the city and eleven adjacent parishes: Oadby, Wigston, Blaby, Nar-
borough, Kirby Muxloe, Groby, Anstey, Birstall, Syston, Scraptoft, and Thurnby.[1]
The more recent of these definitions is the most refined that has yet been attempted.
It comprises the present County Borough of Leicester, the two Urban Districts of
Oadby and Wigston, with sixty-seven parishes lying outside them, from Barrow-
on-Soar to Smeeton Westerby, from Billesdon to Markfield.[2] The boundary runs

[1] *Leicester and Leicestershire Sub-Regional Planning Study* (1969), i. 18.
[2] *Towards a Strategy for the Future. Preliminary Structure Plan Proposals for Leicester and
Leicestershire* (1972), 28, 70.

approximately in a circle with a radius of eight miles from the centre of Leicester. The purpose of the study in which this definition was put forward was to offer the outline of a development plan for the next twenty years, in which it must be assumed that the population of Greater Leicester will steadily increase. The area adopted had therefore to be 'large enough to absorb the scale of growth envisaged by 1991 whatever the form or direction that growth might take'. Although it is no part of the purpose of this book to predict the future, here is a consideration that must be recognised as important. Taking everything into account, this definition of Greater Leicester may be accepted as the most satisfactory one yet put forward.

The population of this district in 1966 was 476,300. To this total the County Borough of Leicester contributed 283,300 – only 59·5 per cent. So that the city proper, at the end of its life as an independent organ of government, included only three-fifths of the population of the whole urban area of which it was the historic centre. When the development of Greater Leicester began, in the Victorian age, the ancient borough – already much enlarged – was by far the most populous section of the whole complex: the outer parts were no more than modest suburbs. Now the suburbs themselves have begun to take over. If the present tendency continues, 'Leicester' – as it has been studied in this book – will before very long account for no more than half the people living in the whole extended city: less than half, perhaps, by the end of the century. And – again depending on the continuance or reversal of present trends – its economic functions, in trade, industry, and employment, may also have diminished in proportion.

These are problems that confront those who are planning for the future. They are among the great question-marks that hang over the City of Leicester at the moment when the old political organism is dissolved. To any one who has looked closely at its history there is in that dissolution something appropriate, and also something puzzling. It is appropriate because it represents an effort, realistic and long overdue, to break down the barriers imposed by the urban boundary: barriers that were always certain to be unreal, however intelligently they were drawn, that seldom at the best corresponded for long to economic or social realities and often in fact denied them. The merger into District and County represents, in this sense, the salutary acceptance of fact. And if, in the long run, it helps to diminish the tension that has often been felt since the seventeenth century between city and county, it will on that account alone have rendered a useful service.

There is something curious here, nevertheless. We live – it is a tedious *cliché* – in an urbanised world. Most of us are townees, though with our liking for seedy euphemism we may call ourselves urban dwellers. Yet have we much sense of the town as such, and do we care for it? On the evidence of what has been happening in Leicester during the past century, it can be said that the suburbs, the outer accretions and growths of the town, are taking it over: a process embodied in symbolic form in the handsome and impressive new County Hall, erected in the suburb of Glenfield (Plate 24b). Is this perhaps a sign – not only in Leicestershire, but in the country at large – that, while we busy ourselves so much with what we call 'urban', we are beginning to forget the town itself, the historic community, to relegate it unconsciously to the lumber-room of history? If so, we are in danger of killing one of the roots of our civilisation. A town like Leicester, with so venerable and lively a past, has a great deal to contribute, in habit and experience, to the changing society of our time. We must hope that under the new system of local government it will be enabled to make that contribution, fully and freely, to the utmost.

V

The Past in the Present

When the Borough of Leicester was incorporated in 1589, it took as its device the badge of the Beaumont Earls, which it had already used for a long time past; and that cinquefoil placed on a red ground, its petals differenced with ermine, has continued as the distinctive and elegant emblem of the town ever since. Nothing could have been more appropriate, as a reminder of the exceptional lordship that had once prevailed in Leicester. When the Borough took a motto, it was that of the great Queen herself who had granted the charter: *Semper Eadem*, Always the Same. That has proved no less apposite: as a reference to the rule of the Tudors, which succeeded the medieval lordship, and more deeply as a reflection of one important aspect of the town itself.

A student of heraldry is apt to look at the arms borne by local government authorities with amusement or disapproval. But in the case of Leicester he must allow that they are singularly apt. Surely no English town can display a motto that summarises so much of its character with equal truth. It outdoes all modern inventions, like Cheltenham's *Salubritas et Eruditio*, or *Filey et Felicitas*.

The words *Semper Eadem* can be taken in two different ways: to emphasise either constancy or conservatism. Both, as we have seen, have been readily discernible in the history of Leicester. The jokers have, of course, made play with the second meaning: fairly enough sometimes, as one was bound to think when one saw the words emblazoned on the sides of the clanking tramcars, nearing their end in the 1940s. But the first sense of the motto cuts deeper, applied to a city that has a history extending over 2000 years and is influenced and moulded by that history even in the daily life of the twentieth century. Street plan, street names, the Market Place and the business transacted there, the relationship of the city to its neighbourhood, its position in the network of communications: all these things, and many more, are intelligible only in the light of the past. That does not determine the life of the present – if it did, the town would be dead, and it is very much alive; but it is a constant influence, at one time perhaps cumbersome, at another ennobling, always there and a force to be reckoned with.

In physical terms, this spirit emerges from the story told in the preceding chapters. Here, in conclusion, a more difficult task must be attempted: to seize something of the character of the city as it appears to us today, in the light of its long evolution. We now move, necessarily, into the realm of opinion, conjecture, prejudice, perhaps even passion; but nowhere, it is to be hoped, beyond evidence and reason.

I

During the past three centuries, Leicester has become one of the leading industrial cities of England. If one surveys the whole of that span of years, and glances further back into remoter time, the story seems to be characterised by two things that stand out from the rest: even continuity and smallness of scale.

The continuity is obvious. When great changes have occurred at single moments of time, as when the religious houses were dissolved in the sixteenth century or the old Corporation in the nineteenth, they have been bloodless; and the new order has been erected on the old. The men coming into power have not refused to build on the foundations laid by the predecessors they displaced.

At first sight it may seem odd to emphasise smallness of scale as a principal element in the making of a town of nearly 300,000 people. But the element is clear beyond mistake. Each of the leading industries that have given Leicester its place in the economy of the modern world emerges slowly from very small beginnings. Their story is one of gradual evolution. In hosiery the process is spread over two generations (cf. i.96–8). We can reject the dramatic story of the inception of the boot and shoe manufacture, and see the industry growing quite slowly instead, in approximately the years 1840–70 (pp. 2–3). As for engineering, its origins go back plainly to James Cort and the little foundries of the late eighteenth century, though the engineering trades do not come to play any striking part in the town's economy until the close of the nineteenth. And each of the branches for which Leicester engineering has come to be well known – such as quarrying machinery, or lifts, or precision instruments, or typewriters – takes its rise from a family business (pp. 4–5).

There, indeed, is the chief clue to it all: the firm based on the family, and the relationship of one family with another. There is nothing unique here. One has only to think of the Rathbones, Gladstones, and Croppers of Liverpool, the

Gurneys and Colmans of Norwich. But family businesses like those were on a quite different scale from that of the firms we meet with in Leicester. They belonged to the national, even the international world of commerce. Their leaders were M.P.s and the advisers of governments. They were — so far as England has ever had such people — merchant princes.

There have been no merchant princes in Leicester. Consider, as one simple test, the fortunes that leading citizens left when they died. Who are the outstanding industrial and commercial men of the town: Leicester's equivalent of the Rathbones and the Gurneys? The two Ellises, Chairmen of the huge Midland Railway? John Ellis left under £40,000 in 1862, his son Edward Shipley a little more than twice that sum in 1879. The largest fortune left by any Victorian Mayor of Leicester was Israel Hart's, at just over £190,000, in 1911. The largest made by anybody connected with the town in the nineteenth century was probably that of John Mason Cook, Thomas Cook's son, who left £623,000. But when he died in 1899 he had long moved away from Leicester. His fortune was made in London and, quite literally, in the whole world.[1]

The leading wealthy citizens of Victorian Leicester left estates expressed in five figures, not in six. The houses they built for themselves in Stoneygate accord exactly with their fortunes. None of them is really large; few have anything about them that is ostentatious; none contained a library or a collection of pictures of any note. That is not inconsistent with a quiet and genuine cultural life, with agreeable painting in watercolours and sound architecture. But it is all, through and through, small in scale.

The small scale has the merits of the economy of thrift. Could any community have got better value, for a little more than £100 a year, than Leicester did from Joseph Dare's Domestic Mission? Can any town show more effective expenditure on public buildings than Leicester's £53,000 on the Town Hall in 1876 or its £21,000 on the De Montfort Hall forty years later?

There is, as we have seen, nothing grand in the history of Leicester, until one reaches back into the remote past, to the fourteenth century and beyond; and then the grandeur has about it something of the external, almost of the accidental. That is true both of the town's buildings and streets and of the men and women who lived in them. The church of the Newarke — now totally destroyed — was probably the most beautiful building that ever stood in Leicester. But its distinction derived from the coherence of its design and from the monuments it contained: not from its size, for it was evidently small (i.52). Everything else in the city is on the same modest scale. It has no street that can be compared with Friargate in Derby; no

[1] There is a mystery about the will of Thomas Cook himself (cf. i.157). When he died in 1892 he left only £2,497: a sum insufficient to discharge even the legacies set down in his will. This surely cannot represent his true fortune.

centre like Northampton's, pivoting on the shapely church of All Saints; nothing spectacular like the Castle rock at Nottingham. Least of all can it show anything to equal the ascent of the steps at Coventry, under the noble portico that links the new cathedral with the old, the walk between St Michael's glorious spire and the Georgian houses of Priory Row.

The dramatic has no place at all in the streets of Leicester. There is little enough of it, as we have seen, anywhere in the town's history. Nothing in the site induces it: slopes and broad terraces rising gently from the Soar, itself a placid – the unkind might call it a sluggish – stream. The one small touch of excitement that the city can offer is the view of Charnwood Forest, forming the skyline half-a-dozen miles away to the north-west; and that is visible only from the highest of those terraces, from the cemetery and the Victoria Park. Those who crave the picturesque and have little sense of history will never care much for Leicester. They will always find it undistinguished.

Nor are they wholly wrong. The town lacks fine buildings. It also lacks outstanding men. No native of Leicester has ever made a great name for himself. Only one citizen has ever been heard of all over the world, Thomas Cook; but he was born in Derbyshire and did not come to live and work in Leicester until he was grown up. In earlier ages truly great men were connected with the town: the second Beaumont Earl, the first Duke of Lancaster. Neither of them was a native, however, or resided in Leicester for long. They both had possessions there, with special powers and responsibilities; but though, in loose language, Leicester might be said to belong to them, they never belonged to it. The same is true of the town's other illustrious lord, the Elizabethan Earl of Huntingdon. Generously careful though he was of the town's welfare, Ashby-de-la-Zouch was his home, not Leicester, and he spent the most important part of his life at York, as Lord President of the Council of the North. In later times, though the borough might occasionally boast a distinguished Member of Parliament, like Ramsay Mac-Donald, no close connection was established between those Members and their constituents, and they influenced the town hardly at all.

The economic activities of the place produced no great men either. Its historic industry is one that might almost be said, for various reasons, to discourage anything of the kind. Nowhere in Britain has the hosiery trade thrown up a man of high national distinction, whether as capitalist, technician, or leader of labour: no Bright or Chamberlain, no Maudslay or Whitworth, no Thomas Burt.

Nevertheless, there is a certain unreality in this line of argument. What has just been said could be said of many others towns – indeed of the majority, of Leicester's size and kind, in England: so that local patriots in Nottingham feel obliged to talk of Kirke White and Festus Bailey, in Sheffield of Ebenezer Elliott. The emergence of individual greatness, of outstanding distinction, must always be rare and accidental. Of the six really eminent men born in Leicestershire during the past five centuries, five sprang from small villages, Brooksby, Fenny Drayton, Lindley, Rothley, Thurcaston; only one, the Marquess of Hastings, was connected with an aristocratic dynasty.

The truth about Leicester in this connection is subtler and more interesting. Though the great may be absent from a society of this kind, even during a very long history, there may still be distinction on a more modest scale: able men produced by the town or coming to live in it to make their own contribution to its life and wealth. Judged by these standards, which are the right standards to take, one can see a good many people who deserve high and continuing respect; more than might generally be supposed. A few of those born in Leicester may be recalled, by way of example. They may perhaps help a little in this quest for the elusive character of the town.

We must disregard a number of medieval writers who bore the name 'de Leicester', since it is usually uncertain how that attribution arose.[1] Considering its strong Protestantism, it is surprising that the town threw up no Puritan divine of the first rank; but in Lazarus Seaman it produced a distinguished one, stamped plainly in the mould of Leicester. He became Master of Peterhouse and Vice-Chancellor of Cambridge under the Interregnum, and then, when his party had been defeated in 1660, recommended and exemplified an attitude of 'silent patience'. He was spoken of with respect for his learning even by the cross-grained Anthony Wood. He assembled a library of over 5,000 books, which is thought to have been the first ever to be sold in England by auction, on his death in London in 1676.[2] Another Cambridge don born in Leicester, of a different stamp, was Richard Farmer, Master of Emmanuel, who wrote a remarkable *Essay on the Learning of Shakespeare* (though almost nothing else) and was deferentially consulted by Dr Johnson. He too was a bibliophile.[3]

The town produced some notable men in the nineteenth century, in quite other fields than these. They all made their fortunes outside Leicester. William Inman, son of a partner in the firm of Pickford's who looked after its business in the town, perceived very early the potential of the iron screw steamship for the Atlantic trade and established in 1850 what became known as the Inman Line. He paid special attention to improving the conditions in which emigrants made the voyage and so, as a fellow-shipowner put it, 'conferred a boon worthy of re-

[1] Cf. J. C. Russell, *Dictionary of Writers of the Thirteenth Century* (1936), 67, 105, 125, 139, 196.

[2] A copy of the catalogue, with the prices marked in it, is at the BM: 821 i. 1.

[3] There is a highly entertaining account of Farmer, written by Nichols (who knew him) in his *Literary Anecdotes* (1812–15), ii. 618–49.

membrance on myriads of poor people'.[1] John Henry Chamberlain became perhaps the leading architect in the redevelopment of Birmingham under Joseph Chamberlain (to whom he was not related). He received his training as an articled pupil of Henry Goddard. His only conspicuous work in his native town, the Hollings Memorial Column at the Museum, was recently demolished. Finally, we should recall two distinguished pupils of the Wyggeston Boys' School: Sir Basil Mott, who became the partner successively of J. H. Greathead and Sir Benjamin Baker, did much to develop the tube railways of London in the 1890s, and was responsible for the Mersey road tunnel of 1934; and E. Phillips Oppenheim, who described himself modestly as 'just a yarn-spinner', but whose spinning gave pleasure to scores of thousands of readers for nearly half a century.[2]

Many of the most interesting men who have emerged from Leicester do not stand as individuals in isolation, but as members of families who together contributed much to the town's well-being and advancement. The Vaughan-Halford clan is an outstanding case. Its founder Dr James Vaughan, a successful physician in Leicester, had seven sons, including a Judge, a Dean, a Minister to the United States, and a President of the Royal College of Physicians. Four members of the family were Vicars of St Martin's in Leicester, of whom one became a celebrated Headmaster of Harrow and another (cf. p. 27) rendered outstanding service to his native town. Such names as Gimson, Goddard, Ellis, Biggs, Herrick, Wyggeston stand for a great deal. Collectively and individually they were important, not only in their town but, many of them, far beyond it.

In the twentieth century the contribution of the family to the life of the town has been extended in a new way: through the participation of women in the city's public life. The first women magistrates were appointed to the Leicester Bench in 1920, the first two women Councillors (Mrs Ellen Swainston and Miss Emily Fortey) were elected in 1922–3. Since then five women have served as Lord Mayors. Miss E. R. Frisby was the first, in 1941–2, and then in 1960–7 came a rapid sequence, in which four out of seven were women. Mrs Irene Pollard has served continuously as Chairman of the Housing Committee for the last eight years of the Council's life. These are appropriate signs of the influence of women in a community in whose economic life they have played an especially notable part.

We are back once more at the family, the unit that has dominated so much of the history of Leicester. For even today, when the economic life of the city has largely passed out of the hands of the families that so long controlled it, the old practices and habits of thinking continue. The business firms of the city still tend

[1] W. S. Lindsay, *History of Merchant Shipping and Ancient Commerce*, iv (1876), 255.
[2] All the men who are mentioned here by name will be found in the *Dictionary of National Biography*.

to look to Leicester itself for the services they need. An investigation by sampling, made about 1970, showed for instance that nearly three-quarters of the Leicester firms insured themselves with companies having branches in the city, whereas in the East Midlands as a whole only just over half the firms did their business locally. In the same way, 83 per cent of the Leicester firms employed local accountants, where the figure for the region as a whole was 63 per cent. Nor are these instances isolated. A similar pattern is to be seen in a whole range of other services, such as advertising and freight broking; and Leicester firms showed an exceptional preference for local lawyers and architects too.[1]

2

Any one who finds Leicester dull must take account not only of such men as those we have just been considering but of others, of a different sort. The place has attracted, in a quite remarkable degree, the interest and affection of a long succession of serious students – with the result that its history today is perhaps as well recorded as that of any comparable town in England. Burton, Staveley, and Carte began the work, followed by Throsby and Nichols, who systematised and developed it. In the early Victorian age Thompson and Kelly turned their attention to the borough records, not only using them to enrich the social history in their own books but generously bestowing time and intelligence on caring for the documents themselves. Then, in the 1890s, the Corporation was persuaded to underwrite the printing of a substantial selection from the records.[2] It entrusted the task to Mary Bateson, whose work could scarcely have been better performed. We now have four volumes more, with two others containing the Freemen's Register – that 'great catalogue of the obscure'[3] – and a biographical dictionary of the Mayors and Lord Mayors from 1209 to 1935.

At the same time the physical remains and the topography of the medieval town were being studied afresh, largely under the guidance of Hamilton Thompson. It is still a profitable education to walk round the ancient churches with his descriptions in one's hand, following from one stone and window to another that benign and vigilant eye. And no one who lives in the city today with any feeling for its more distant past can do without Charles Billson's *Medieval Leicester*, an exemplary piece of topographical analysis.

Just before and after the Second World War a new influence made itself felt, that of W. G. Hoskins, another true topographer, imaginatively exploiting new

[1] *Office Services in the East Midlands*, 49.
[2] *Council Minutes*, 1895–6, 104–5, 296–300.
[3] W. G. Hoskins, *Provincial England* (1963), 76.

sources of knowledge, for example in wills and inventories. Leicester is indebted to him not only for what he himself wrote about it but also for the writing he directed and inspired. The resumed publication of the *Victoria County History*, from 1954 onwards, was due above all to his editorial work. And it was at his insistence that the entire fourth volume of that *History* was devoted to the city of Leicester – with results that every student will profit from for very many years to come.

Even this does not exhaust the tale. When A. T. Patterson's *Radical Leicester* appeared in 1954, it was at once recognised as an outstandingly full and careful account of the growth of an industrial town. And, side by side with these works of scholarship, Leicester has been the subject of a series of more popular studies, interpreting old and new knowledge to a larger audience: among them Mrs Fielding Johnson's *Glimpses of Ancient Leicester*, a much-loved book, liberally illustrated and written largely for the schoolchildren of the town; S. H. Skillington's history, crisp, elegant, and clear, like all he wrote; and Colin Ellis's *History in Leicester*, original in method and most competently executed. The last of these is unlike all its predecessors, in that its author had written not only history but also verse, and there is here and there a poetic quality to be discerned in the book that sets it, in this company, apart. He never published a poem about Leicester itself, but his 'Living in the Midlands' expresses something of his feeling for Leicestershire, of which he wrote delightfully elsewhere.[1] Its concluding stanza can be applied as much to the city of Leicester as to the county:

> And we who set out to discover
> The charms of my county can be
> As proud as a plain woman's lover
> Of beauties the world does not see.[2]

That wry-faced affection – reticent, critical, yet deeply sincere – is a feeling that has characterised many of those who have come to know and appreciate Leicester at its true worth.

The town, then, has attracted much intelligent study, from people of widely different kinds, over the past three centuries. The explanation lies not in the mere length of its history, but in its rich texture, which alone makes such study rewarding. And perhaps we can take another hint here from Colin Ellis's poem. May it not be that one thing that has, even unconsciously, drawn these students to it has been the very fact that it is not obviously romantic, that its interest needs to be dug out from beneath the covering drawn over it by modern workaday life?

That is symbolised to perfection in the plan of the city's centre today. Two of the chief arteries of its business, Gallowtree Gate and Charles Street, lie outside the

---

[1] For Colin Ellis cf. 45 TLAS (1969–70) 68–73.
[2] *Mournful Numbers* (1932), 23.

Old Town altogether. Of the other two, High Street is a dreary rebuilding of seventy years ago; and the new Inner Ring Road has nothing whatever to do with the streets or buildings of any earlier age – with the sole exception of the Magazine Gateway, which it engulfs and renders foolish. It is quite pardonable that the visitor, coming into Leicester or driving through it, should suppose it to be a wholly modern town; less pardonable, but almost as common, to find citizens supposing the same thing. Few historic cities, not subjected to the martyrdom of large-scale bombing, can seem to ignore their past so resolutely. And yet on the other hand Leicester has occasionally shown a tenderness, even a touch of imagination, in the care of its historic inheritance.

This is a town capable of inspiring affection: not romantic devotion, such as one might feel for Wells or Lincoln if one were fortunate enough to live there, but the plain matter-of-fact liking that Colin Ellis hints at. It is pre-eminently a comfortable place to be in, clean – as such towns go, in the filthy and wasteful world of the 1970s – and, in some respects at least, notably well run. It is a town well endowed with parks and recreation grounds – nearly twenty in all, half-a-dozen of them large; well planted with trees and happy in a long tradition of gardening, public and private. The Leicester clay is cruel to work, but it yields an abundance of roses.

Professor Hoskins – no native himself, though a resident for twenty years – once described the city thus:

> Solid, Victorian, brick-built and prosaic, Leicester . . . has a small-town homeliness (for all its 300,000 people), a comfortable feeling of Sunday dinners and security, of chapels and libraries and much earnest winter reading and lecturing, of life still revolving around 'the old Clock Tower' as it did in grandfather's time, that many of us find appealing and satisfying in a world that is increasingly buried in soulless concrete: a delightful Betjeman town that one would not willingly see too much changed.[1]

Those words were written in the mid-1950s, and they speak for many of us, loudly and clearly, still. But some people, superstitiously inclined, might feel that they invited the very calamity they deplored: for they had not been published long before the invasion of concrete got under way. In the 'sixties, as we saw in Chap. III, the pace became fast, and the change that Professor Hoskins feared soon began to render much of the city he was describing unrecognisable.

One is left to wonder how far, in these matters, Leicester can remain true to its past, or will wish to do so. Clearly it must come to terms with the present: but those terms need not be an unconditional surrender. How far do the people of Leicester realise what is at stake? Perhaps not many of them regard the city with real pride. Its good qualities are not those that one boasts about. It is seldom the

[1] W. G. Hoskins, *Leicestershire* (1957), 133.

biggest in anything, or the first to produce an innovation; nobody could call it picturesque. Plain comfort has nothing to do with glory. But, for most communities, it is a more sensible ideal to pursue; and Leicester has pursued it, in a quiet way, throughout most of its history.

3

No Leicester man has ever made a national reputation in politics. The reason is suggested, tersely and shrewdly, by Mr Evans, the best historian of the town's modern political life: 'It may be that Leicester was too independent, its spirit too egalitarian, its resources too evenly distributed to produce or tolerate the counterpart of a Joseph Chamberlain'.[1] Once it looked like doing so, when John Biggs – a Radical capitalist, too – made his way forward in the 1840s and 1850s. But Biggs was destroyed by his own virtues and faults, as well as by the jealousy of his fellow-Radicals; and Leicester has seen no one like him, before or since.

The town has long been suspicious of political leadership. The explanation of that is plain in its history. Though it never embarked on a battle with its medieval lords, it had more than once good reason to rue their dominion; and when the third Earl of Huntingdon died in 1595 it extricated itself deftly from the influence of his weak successors. In the seventeenth century, both for better and for worse, the town's affairs passed decisively under its own control, except for a short time in the 1680s, when the volatile interference of the royal government left behind it nothing but a fervent determination to keep even closer control, once that had been regained. At the same time the town came to resent the political influence that neighbouring landlords tried to exercise there. And so the tight oligarchy developed that retained power until 1836 – to be displaced then by what was in many respects only another oligarchy, operating in a different political sense. The emergence of even a limited democracy was a very gradual process, spread over the next eighty years.

Through all these mutations, one thing is constant: the absence of any outstanding leader. No matter what political banner they fought under, Tories, Radicals, Liberals, Labour men, all agreed in rejecting the dominance of any individual. The self-perpetuating Tory Council of the 1820s was in this respect just as jealously egalitarian as the Trades Council seventy years later.

Not was it solely a matter of politics. The prevailing religious tone in Leicester had exactly the same tendency. If the Anglican church was dominant for the 300 years following the Reformation, its supremacy was accepted on very special terms, which were dictated first by Henry Earl of Huntingdon and then by the Corpora-

[1] VCHL iv. 250.

tion. This 'municipal Anglicanism' — such it might fairly be called — was doctrinally Calvinist, and firm in the control it exercised over the town's clergy. The Corporation not only paid preachers and helped to support the impecunious vicars of St Martin's, the pre-eminently civic church; it came to augment the meagre stipends of all the other livings too.[1] But in resolving to do so it was careful to say that its contribution would be paid 'during pleasure'. None of the clergymen it assisted in this way after the Restoration was bold enough to incur its displeasure, with the obvious consequence that would entail.

The parson's freehold (a concept to which England has owed a great deal in its history) bore a modified meaning in Leicester; for the freehold, by itself, in most of the churches there was worth very little. Inevitably the Anglican clergyman came to be dependent in large measure on the goodwill of his congregation, as the Nonconformist minister was entirely. Only a big man like Thomas Robinson, Vicar of St Mary de Castro, could stand up to a bully on the Corporation.[2] Even when those days had passed, Canon Vaughan, strong though he was both personally and socially, owed much of the very limited ascendancy he attained in the town to his far-seeing liberalism, his care for the working classes, not in any sense to a spiritual dominance; and the obloquy he endured for a time as the first Chairman of the Leicester School Board[3] arose in part from the Nonconformists' jealousy of the Establishment, their eagerness to cut a dangerous Anglican priest down to size.

As for the Nonconformists, who became so powerful an element in the life of Leicester, all their thinking tended in the same direction, with their emphasis — varying from one sect to another — upon the independence of the congregation and the elective nature of the ministry. Robert Hall is the only Dissenting minister of Leicester who ever attained eminence,[4] and though his reputation arose in the main from his eloquent preaching, it was due in part to his fearless and compassionate liberalism: a liberalism associated, like Vaughan's later in the century, with the improvement of the life of the working classes.

4

All these arguments seem to tend in one direction: towards mediocrity, throned and crowned. But the consequences are not, in fact, so simple. Granted that there were no outstanding political and social leaders in Leicester, able to carry opinion

[1] Cf. for example RBL v. 25, 76, 145, 160, 255.
[2] E. T. Vaughan, *Account of the Rev. Thomas Robinson* (1815), 64–7.
[3] 33 TLAS (1957) 53.
[4] Disregarding those who stayed in the town only a very short time, like the missionary and Orientalist William Carey, and Edward Miall, the protagonist of Disestablishment.

along with them and mould it, yet unobtrusive guidance, intelligently applied and accepted, could still play its part and prevail. There are no figures in Leicester's cultural life in the least comparable with William Roscoe in Liverpool or Sir William Burrell in Glasgow. And yet, by the common consent of those who are able to judge, the museums of Leicester came to stand among the first half-dozen in the provinces of Great Britain, distinguished in number, in scope, and in quality.[1] How can this have occurred?

To begin with, as we have seen (i.172–3), the municipality was quick to avail itself of the first Museums Act, of 1845, and the strongest cultural institution in the town, the Literary and Philosophical Society, came forward with the offer of its collections; the two bodies, public and private, acting together in a spirit of cautious enlightenment. In the Mid-Victorian age the Museum, like most of its fellows elsewhere, developed very slowly; but it was enlarged, again by a combination of municipal and private action, in 1876, and a well-directed expansion began with the appointment of Montagu Browne as Curator in 1880. He and most of his successors have been notable men. The Corporation chose their servants well, supported them steadily, and – the vital thing – accepted their advice.

The consequences for the city's well-being have ranged far beyond what a museum is conventionally thought to be concerned with. All the most important of the city's old buildings, except the churches, are now in the Museums' capable keeping.[2] Some – Belgrave Hall, the Magazine Gateway, the Museum of Costume – have been preserved from destruction almost wholly by their efforts. Their Archives Department is responsible for the publication of the records of the town, to an admirable and original plan. Their Schools Service was early in the field and has long been highly reputed; its work has not stopped at the city boundary. The Museums themselves – nine of them, new and old – offer between them boundless instruction and pleasure. And at the heart of them all stands the original Museum in New Walk, appropriately housed in a building first devoted to education, a classical building that rejected 'the dark monastic exploded institutions of our country'.[3] That Museum has always been a point at which past and present have shaken hands.

[1] It is worth adding that, with the exception of Brighton – which is a quite special case, owing to the Corporation's responsibility for the Royal Pavilion, a minor national monument – all the other towns with which Leicester could be compared in this respect were very much larger.

[2] To be exact, the Jewry Wall is in the hands of the national Government; but the day-to-day charge of it falls to the City Museums.

[3] The phrase is the Mayor's, in his speech at the opening of the building as the Proprietory School in 1837 (q. M. Seaborne, *The English School: its Architecture and Organisation*, 1971, 188). One cannot help wondering how the architect of the building, Joseph Hansom, who was a Roman Catholic, relished it.

Here then is one case — others could be cited too — in which the corporate body was prepared to accept leadership and guidance, with an impressive result; but on condition that the leadership and guidance sprang from its own servants, not from any one who might wish to become its master. The story is worth considering, at a time when the committee system in local government is, often most reasonably, under fire.

So a valuable kind of leadership can after all emerge in modern Leicester, in the face of much that is particularly adverse to it. And one positive thing must be said, in praise of the spirit that has so long predominated in the town. At its best, it can attain ethical refinement and great moral force. Again, let us take a single example.

John Ellis is one of the few Leicester men to find a place in the *Dictionary of National Biography*. Farmer, grazier, corn factor, Quaker, he turned his attention to quarrying, and that led him into railway development. When the Midland Railway Company was formed in 1844, the first of the great railway amalgamations, he became Vice-Chairman under George Hudson. Hudson's enormous financial malpractices brought him to ruin four years later, whereupon Ellis took over from him. It required a strong nerve and courage to face the angry tumult of investors who had lost so much: for he was not a saviour who had been brought in from outside, he had occupied the second place in the Company throughout. Yet no one seriously suggested that he had lent himself to anything fraudulent. Furious and frightened as they were, the shareholders accepted his rule, and he carried them through to safety in the 'fifties. It was a formidable task, which lay near the centre of the economic life of Britain, and he achieved it by a combination of business shrewdness, total integrity, and resolution — all at the service of a quiet and unshakeable moral power. That combination of qualities reflects his faith, and his town, at their best.

5

Like most other towns that have any character at all, Leicester is celebrated for some distinctions to which it really has little or no claim. Certain clichés are constantly applied to it. We are told, again and again, that it is one of the cleanest cities in the United Kingdom. That statement may well have been true in the later Victorian age, when the Council exercised a firm control over the emission of smoke from factory chimneys; and Leicester was always fortunate in that the nearest coalfield was ten miles and more away. The atmosphere was indeed relatively clear. Visitors to the city were constantly surprised to find that on many days they could look across it over a cluster of chimneys to see the hills of Charnwood Forest. And yet, when the atmosphere of Leicester was scientifically examined in 1937–9, it turned out to be somewhat cleaner than that of the great manufacturing towns of the North or of Stoke-on-Trent, but more polluted than, for example, Cardiff's – where a different type of coal was burnt.[1]

Again, Leicester is often alleged to be a city of migrants, of people in transit through it, coming there to work and then passing on. This is a statement impossible to accept or disprove, since the statistics are not available. But in the years for which we have some information (1851–1911: cf. p. 151), about three-quarters of the population of the town had been born there or within Leicestershire; and at the close of that period the proportion was gently rising. A great immigration certainly took place after the Second World War, reinforced by the influx from overseas, which was on an unusually large scale. Leicester has perhaps attracted more of these recent immigrants than some of its neighbours; but it is a mere matter of assertion that the number of the citizens born in the city is proportionately smaller than elsewhere.

Or again, it has been a commonplace to consider the town as dominated, to an exceptional degree, by Nonconformity: so much so that it will seem at least perverse, perhaps heretical, to question this assumption. It contains elements of undoubted truth. There is no mistaking where the citizens' sympathies, broadly, lay during the Civil War. They showed no enthusiasm for the restored monarchy or Church; they were quick to establish and multiply Dissenting conventicles when they had the opportunity. The ablest and most enterprising hosiery manufacturers were, in general, Nonconformists; and the Church of England lost, as well as the Tory party, by the political reforms of 1832–5. Yet odd facts stand out obstinately on the other side: the backwardness of the Dissenters in promoting education (i.174–5); the strength of certain Anglican clergymen, like Carte (i.106–7) and Robinson (i.177–8) and Vaughan (p. 27 above), which was every whit as great as that of any Nonconformist, even Robert Hall; the failure of the Nonconformists to fill their meeting-houses, as we see from the census of 1851; the frequency with which those meeting-houses came and went, contrasted with the steady (if slow) increase in the provision of churches by the Establishment. Liberalism enjoyed a total and unchanging supremacy in Leicester between 1836 and 1914. We have seen how it moulded the political and social development of the town. Its religious counterpart, Protestant Dissent, has left no corresponding imprint behind, no comparable memorials of constructive achievement. Though many of its ministers rendered quiet good service to the town, none of them after Mursell can really be said to have earned remembrance as a leader of thought or

[1] *Atmospheric Pollution in Leicester: a Scientific Survey* (1945), 124–5.

action. The influence of the Dissenting bodies over the modern town has tended to be negative; it has seldom been a positive, inspiring force.

And yet, in a subtle and hidden way, it has made one great contribution, which has not perhaps been appreciated as it should be. There is eternally, in Miall's phrase, a 'dissidence of Dissent', a predilection for wrangling that springs from the very origin of Dissent itself and is apt to expand into a general quarrelsomeness, congregation against minister, sect against sect. These things exhibit themselves amply in Leicester, again and again, during the past three or four centuries. But though the war of words has often been noisy and bitter (even more often, tediously verbose), it has nevertheless remained an argument, an effort to persuade by reason, not by brute force; and the argument has often ended by achieving sensible compromise.

The society of this town, as we have examined it, has shown some qualities of long continuance. It has lacked resident magnates; it has never been under the power of millionaires, or dominated by a single great commercial corporation; the workers and their employers have quarrelled fiercely at times, yet their interests were in large measure interdependent; women were almost as directly involved in the fluctuating fortunes of the town as their menfolk. All these things made it a closely-knit community, conducting its affairs by a process of argument, not by dictation and violence. If the quarrels of Dissenters have often rendered their influence nugatory, Dissent stands, at its best, upon an appeal to reason. That appeal has often succeeded in Leicester, and there is one underlying cause of its relatively fortunate history. On this account it owes a debt beyond assessment to the tenacity and the moderating force of the Nonconformist tradition.

6

Where now, finally, shall one turn to seize the spirit of this city, so often disparaged, or patronised, or misunderstood?

If one thinks Nonconformity is its chief element, then it must surely be to the Great Meeting, which embodies still in secluded dignity so much of the long history of Dissent, of argument and reason that have often in the end prevailed, of sound and intelligent charity. But the situation of the Great Meeting is now forlorn, facing on to a huge empty space cleared by demolition, surrounded by buildings that will soon meet a similar fate. It is as a lodge in a garden of cucumbers, as a besieged city. The Great Meeting can exemplify the past, but scarcely the present or the future.

Or one might go to the Clock Tower. It has been the butt of many jokes in the past hundred years, and even the most ardent latter-day Victorian must allow it has the quality of the preposterous. But its statues do in fact recall to us much of the history of Leicester, though not always perhaps for the reasons that were in the minds of those who commissioned them: education and well-directed charity again, commercial enterprise, and in Simon de Montfort — not indeed a Father of Liberty, but a powerful representative of the peculiar dominion under which the borough lived in the Middle Ages. Here too, however, we are looking back, not forward: for the Clock Tower itself is ceasing to be a focal point of traffic, to become hardly more than a monument at the centre of an irregular polygon devoted to pedestrians.

No. We can do better than that by returning to the place where the recorded and visible history of Leicester begins, to stand on the open platform outside the entrance to Vaughan College, facing across the bath site to the Jewry Wall. A Roman monument comparable with that wall is to be found in no other large industrial town in Britain, outside London, and in very few in Europe anywhere north of the Alps. Backed as it is by the Saxon and Norman church of St Nicholas, it is unique: the best symbol that could by any imagination be devised of the Roman origins of our civilisation and the religion that has transfigured it. Behind and beside those living monuments of the old world roars the life of our own time. One road dives under another by a concrete underpass; to the right stands the Holiday Inn, a piece of that Atlantic world to which we owe our survival in the twentieth century. And beside us and beneath our feet is a monument to the genuine education of the spirit, underpinned by enlightened public authority. Here is a museum facing on to an historic site and achieving the rare distinction of becoming an integral part of it. Above it is the College Vaughan founded, developed into something different from what he conceived, but adapting itself to the changes in the social life of our century: a College that still reflects much of the self-improvement that so many people in this city have pursued. Its spirit is indigenous to Leicester, and perfectly stated in the words of St Stephen that Vaughan chose for its motto: 'Sirs, ye are brethren'.

Appendix

POPULATION AND EMPLOYMENT
1851–1971

This table, in continuation of that in i.185, gives the census figures, in so far as they exist, taken from the published returns. Those relating to employment are for men and women aged twenty and more. After 1911 the birthplace figures disappear, and the basis of the employment figures changes so greatly that they cease to be comparable with those that have gone before. The figures in the second column are those given in the first definitive reports issued; some have since been slightly revised.

Year	Population	No. of houses	Persons per house	Percentage born in Leics.	Hosiery men	Hosiery women	Hosiery total	Footwear men	Footwear women	Footwear total	Engineering
1851	60,642	12,816	4·7	80·8	4,188	1,979	6,167	804	589	1,393	
1861	68,056	14,595	4·7	80·5	3,323	1,764	5,087	1,362	953	2,315	
1871	95,220	19,800	4·8	76·6	2,867	1,840	4,707	3,714	1,389	5,103	
1881	122,376	24,973	4·9	74·6	3,121	5,214	8,335	9,172	3,883	13,055	
1891	174,624	29,228	5·9	71·7	4,286	8,381	12,667	16,839	7,320	24,159	1,011
1901	211,579	32,995	6·4	72·5	3,282	9,107	12,389	17,700	8,791	26,491	2,893
1911	227,222	50,940	4·5	73·9	3,610	12,117	15,727	15,715	7,780	23,495	6,410
1921	234,143	53,907	4·3								
1931	239,169	60,719	3·9								
1951	285,181	82,222	3·5								
1961	273,470	88,771	3·0								
1971	284,208	94,365	3·0								

Index

153